THE JOY OF SPINNING

THE JOY
OF SPINNING

Marilyn Kluger

Illustrated by Nanene Queen Jacobson

An Owl Book
HENRY HOLT AND COMPANY   NEW YORK

Copyright © 1971, 1991 by Marilyn Kluger
All rights reserved, including the right to reproduce
this book or portions thereof in any form.
Published by Henry Holt and Company, Inc.,
115 West 18th Street, New York, New York 10011.
Published in Canada by Fitzhenry & Whiteside Limited,
195 Allstate Parkway, Markham, Ontario L3R 4T8.

Library of Congress Cataloging-in-Publication Data
Kluger, Marilyn.
The joy of spinning / by Marilyn Kluger ;
illustrated by Nanene Queen Jacobson.—1st Owl ed., updated ed.
p.   cm.
Includes index.
ISBN 0–8050–1397–0 (alk. paper)
1. Hand spinning.   I. Title.
TT847.K58   1991
746.1–dc20   90–5209
                                                          CIP

Henry Holt books are available at special discounts for bulk purchases for sales
promotions, premiums, fund-raising, or educational use. Special editions or book
excerpts can also be created to specification.

For details contact:
Special Sales Director, Henry Holt and Company, Inc.,
115 West 18th Street, New York, New York 10011.

First published in hardcover by Simon & Schuster in 1971.

First Owl Book Edition—1991
Updated Edition

Printed in the United States of America
Recognizing the importance of preserving the written word,
Henry Holt and Company, Inc., by policy, prints all of its
first editions on acid-free paper. ∞
10 9 8 7 6 5 4 3 2 1

Acknowledgments

My thanks to the first generation of twentieth-century handspinners who read *The Joy of Spinning* during the past twenty-year period. They brought about the revival of spinning as a craft and its establishment as one of the popular fiber arts.

I am grateful to my literary agent, Jane Jordan Browne, and my editor, Tracy Bernstein, for bringing about the "revival" of *The Joy of Spinning* with the publication of this edition. It is gratifying to see continuing interest in the timeless craft of handspinning—and in my book as well.

To Vardine Moore
A spinner of other yarns

Contents

Foreword

A few years ago I went to a craft fair in Gatlinburg, Tennessee, where I watched a lovely lady spinning thread on an old flax wheel.

An excitement I had known as a child returned and I left Gatlinburg re-enchanted with the art of spinning, determined to find my own wheel for spinning.

The search for a spinning wheel was a serendipitous adventure. I finally found a large wool wheel, then a smaller Saxony wheel, then another, and before long I had six spinning wheels that would not work and upon which I could not spin yarn. Furthermore, I could not buy raw wool here in southern Indiana, where sheep are raised on a small scale, because a mysterious entity, known only as the "Wool Pool," promptly consumed all the available fleece.

I learned eventually that a monk in St. Meinrad Archabbey had taught himself to spin. St. Meinrad is fifty-five miles from my home in Newburgh, Indiana, and the prospect of venturing into the monastery was one I considered timidly until I found three other women who shared my interest. Together we made weekly trips to the abbey, where Brother Kim repaired our spinning wheels and shared his knowledge with us.

Our reasons for wanting to spin were various. Mary Jane was restoring a Rappite house in New Harmony, Indiana, and planned to have demonstrations of pioneer crafts in the Epple Haus. Marge was interested in artistic expression and wanted to discover the joy of spinning. Marion was an artist and expert weaver who wanted handspun yarn for her loom. I was interested in needlework and vegetable dyeing, but my own desire was rooted in childhood experiences and became more complex as I became involved with spinning.

In addition, we all were interested in learning to spin as an effort to help preserve the ancient craft of handspinning. I hope to advance this effort by sharing my experiences with others who want to know the joy of spinning.

MARILYN KLUGER

CHAPTER ONE

Spinning Wheels and Goldenrods

One day I came into my grandmother's kitchen and found her sitting beside a spinning wheel, which took sheep's wool from her hand and twisted it, magically, into a long strand of creamy white yarn.

The spool whirled around and around, filling with spun yarn as my grandmother's deft fingers fed long curls of combed wool to the hungry spindle. I watched, spellbound, while the spinning wheel consumed the fleece.

When the basket of combed wool began to empty, Grandmother put the carders in my hands and taught me to pull the bent wire teeth over the tufts of tangled fleece. I was promised a warm woolly cap to wear before the first snowfall if I helped comb fleece to make the yarn.

All afternoon I tugged at the carders, combing out seeds and burrs that had snagged the sheep's coat before shearing time. As Grandmother spun the curls of fleece into yarn for my woolly cap she encouraged me at my task by spinning tales of times past.

Carding the wool, Grandmother said, was how she helped her own grandmother with the task of spinning in the old days. When she was a child the spinning wheel—the very one we were using now—was kept by the hearth. At night the sound of spinning lulled her to sleep. The spinning wheel was seldom quiet, because the great loom, which filled the weaving room upstairs, required endless quantities of thread. Five spinsters spinning one day could provide warp and woof for only one day's weaving. When thread was needed, all the womenfolk of the family worked together to keep the spinning wheel whirling, just as we were doing now, grandmother and grandchild, womenfolk of our family.

The golden thread of my fascination with the art of spinning was spun that afternoon as I combed wool and the wheel turned out yarn for my woolly cap. Grandmother drew out the thread of the past as skillfully as she drew out fleece. I was mesmerized by the cadence of her gentle voice and the music the spinning wheel made. The treadle thumped, the carders scraped, the bobbin whirred, the spinning wheel squeaked as it responded to the rhythm of Grandmother's hand and foot. Into the fleecy strand that wound around the spool was plied an intangible filament of fascination with spinning wheels, which, even then, was weaving itself into the fabric of my years.

When I tired of carding, Grandmother let me try my hand at the wheel. I soon discovered that treadling and spinning, which seemed so easy and effortless as Grandmother did them, were very difficult. I happily returned to carding the wool, which required less coordination and concentration. Grandmother assured me I would get the knack of spinning after a few more tries.

When evening came my hands were soft with lanolin and my arms tired, but I felt pleased and proud that we womenfolk had produced the soft hanks of yarn that were now looped over the wall pegs where Grandfather hung his coat and hat in wintertime. I promised to return the next morning to help wash the wool clean.

I went home filled with new admiration for Grandmother's homey talents, feeling a little sad that spinning, once the daily hearthside occupation of our womenfolk, was now old-fashioned. Even Grandmother kept her spinning wheel in the attic, where it had collected dust since World War I, when she had last spun yarn and knitted stockings and mufflers for her soldier sons.

Now one of those sons, my uncle, had brought her a sackful of fine sheep's wool. It was this odd, nostalgia-evoking gift that had prompted her to bring the wheel down from the attic—the first time in twenty years—to see if she could still spin yarn.

Until I happened into the kitchen that day Grandmother had been spinning sentimental yarn—yarn for which there was no real need. Now I was to have a woolly cap, knitted of this special yarn. I would wear it when the first snowflakes fell, sledding down the white hill behind the barn, a long tail of yellow wool flying behind me, whipping the wind. The scene I saw in my imagination was shamelessly copied from a Christmas greeting I treasured, one I kept in a corner of my mirror to look at on hot summer days when thinking of cold weather was refreshing.

The new words I had heard sang in my ears—distaff, flyer, footman, maiden, rolag, carder, mother-of-all. I skipped home to the rhythm of "niddy noddy, two heads, one body." I could hardly wait until the next day, when I would try my hand at the wheel again. I wanted very much to get the knack of spinning once and for all, to please Grandmother as well as myself.

But the next morning the spinning wheel had been taken from the kitchen and returned to the attic. Enough yarn was spun for one small woolly cap, Grandmother said, and no more knitting yarn was needed.

My disappointment lingered as we prepared soapsuds, of lye soap chips and hot water, to wash the wool. Grandmother sensed my yearning for another try at the wheel and appeased me by supposing that we might spin more yarn after the cap was knitted, enough to tie a comforter, perhaps. Then she sent me to the well with the bucket for drawing up the water.

I promised Grandmother to return to help wash the wool clean.

We poured bucketfuls of soapsuds into a deep washtub outdoors, and cooled it down to lukewarm with clear water drawn from the well. Grandmother rolled up her sleeves and tested the temperature with one elbow. If the water was too hot, she said, the wool would mat and be ruined.

Unwashed wool is uncommonly dirty. As the hanks of dirty yarn sank beneath the suds a barny, wet-animal odor surrounded us. Again and again we squeezed the hanks of wool until the sudsy water was gray, with little blackened curds of soap clinging to the sides of the washtub. Finally the wool came clean.

Then more soft water was drawn from the well for rinsing, and the snowy white yarn was hung out to dry under the backyard shade tree.

When we were finished, my arms ached more than they had the day before. The lanolin softness of my hands had washed away in harsh lye water.

That evening I heard the music of spinning in a minor key. My nose crinkled as I remembered the animal odor of the dirty wet yarn. I hoped my woolly cap would not smell like wet sheep if I tumbled in the snow.

When the wool was dry and fluffy we decided to dye it yellow like the woolly cap worn by the figure on my Christmas card. Grandmother said we could get a pretty shade of yellow from goldenrods, which bloom everywhere in an August countryside, tinting whole fields golden and causing Grandfather to sneeze and sneeze.

While I gathered a basketful of goldenrod florets Grandmother prepared a mordant of alum, cream of tartar, and water, into which she dipped the hanks of spun wool. Without this acid bath the wool yarn might not take the dye.

The yellow dyestuff from my basket was put into a gray granite kettle and covered with soft well water. The kettle boiled all morning on the back of the coal range, filling the kitchen with steam and a peculiar tangy odor. When the color of the water suited Grandmother she set the kettle off the stove to cool. Soon we strained the liquid through cheesecloth into a white dishpan.

The dye liquid was the color of goldenrods with sunlight on them. Into the glistening liquid went the cool, wet hanks of wool that were to become my woolly cap, and the dye pot was returned to the top of the kitchen range.

While the tinted water again heated slowly, Grandmother gently lifted the yarn from the dye with two sticks to see what color we were getting. Gradually the white wool took the color of the dye, and finally, when the water was about to boil, Grandmother hooked the sticks into the loops of the yarn skeins and lifted out the bright yellow yarn for my woolly cap.

Again the skeins of wet wool were hung outside on the clothesline, but this time not in the shade of the maple tree. The blazing August sun would brighten the beautiful goldenrod hue of the yarn while the skeins dripped and dried.

When I returned again the next afternoon the yellow yarn was rolled into balls and put away in the top drawer of the cherry bureau. Grandmother was busy in the kitchen peeling ripe peaches. Steam hovered over the granite kettle we had used yesterday as a dye pot to make color for my woolly cap, but this time peach preserves were cooking.

"The peaches are dead ripe." Grandmother spread butter, then peach preserves, on a thick slice of home-baked bread and handed it to me.

"There will be plenty of time to knit the cap before the first snow flies," she said.

I took the balls of yellow yarn from the bureau drawer. Winter seemed a long way off and waiting was impossible. I draped strands of the yarn around my head and preened in front of the mirror. By standing back across the room and squinting my eyes, I could see the gay yellow woolly cap just as it would be after Grandmother had knitted it.

Even now when I see that particular color of yellow I can see that yellow woolly cap just as clearly as I saw it that day in my grandmother's crackled mirror and in my imagination, where it still exists.

The yellow woolly cap was never knitted. Hot peach preserves scalded Grandmother's hands that August day. A winter's snow fell and melted away before her tender fingers could again perform their tasks without discomfort. Before the snow of another winter lay on the hill beyond the barn other enchantments had pushed the wish for a woolly cap into a corner of my mind.

I forgot the globes of yellow yarn, put away in the bureau drawer like small August suns, until ten more goldenrod-filled summers had faded away. Then, when I was almost a bride, the fragile thread of my fascination with spinning wheels and goldenrods again worked to the top of the cloth to resume its pattern.

Grandmother gave me a down-filled comforter for my bride's dowry. Its patchwork field was made from scraps of Grandmother's dresses—

dark calico prints, small geometric designs, and dainty flower-sprigged cottons. It was a patchwork of memories and reminders, a diary of my childhood in design and pattern, an August meadow strewn with golden-rods. The familiar yellow yarn knotted into the comforter crisscrossed the top like sled tracks in the snow.

"Remember?" Grandmother's fingers touched a yellow tail of yarn. "We made that yarn together a long time ago."

The downy comforter my grandmother made warmed me through the snow-filled winters afterward. Though the gay yellow sprigs of yarn faded and the calico scraps saddened, it became even more pleasing to my eye, softer to touch, and warmer than ever.

The downy comforter my grandmother made warmed me through the snow-filled winters. . . .

CHAPTER TWO

Finding a Spinning Wheel
—with Serendipity

> I once read a silly fairy tale called *The Three Princes of Serendip;* as their Highnesses travelled, they were always making discoveries, by accidents and sagacity, of things which they were not in quest of.
> . . . now do you understand serendipity?
>
> —Horace Walpole in a letter
> to Sir Horace Mann, January 28, 1754

One autumn, when the October wanderlust came on us, my husband and I took our two sons and drove down to Gatlinburg, Tennessee. We knew that there, at the foot of the Smoky Mountains, where the fall foliage is unsurpassed in beauty, the best artisans of the Southern Appalachian Highlands gather together for a five-day Craftsman's Fair. We were hunting for handmade folk-craft items to sell in our old-fashioned Country Store in Newburgh, Indiana. We hoped to meet craftsmen there who would supply us with corn-shuck dolls, handmade brooms, pottery, and handwoven rag rugs.

Along the Ohio River and down through Kentucky, blue October was our bonus. Leaves of sycamore, maple, dogwood, black gum and sassafras had "ripened to the fall" and spiraled down onto the highway, confettilike, because a gentle wind insisted. It was Indian summer, a blue-gold day when summer's hot sun lingers and autumn's cool air arrives, a euphoric meeting that stirs the blood and hides the hilltops under smoky-blue haze. When the humpy outlines of the Great Smoky Mountains appeared on the horizon we understood their name.

19

The Southern Highland Handicraft Guild sponsors the Crafts-man's Fair. The Guild is a nonprofit, educational organization of crafts-men in the mountain areas of Kentucky, Tennessee, the Virginias and Carolinas, Georgia, Maryland, and Alabama which was formed in 1930 to encourage, preserve and improve the traditional and indigenous crafts of the Southern Highlands. The craftsman's fairs held in the summer in Asheville, North Carolina, and in the fall in Gatlinburg, Tennessee, provide opportunity for the exhibition and sale of the crafts of Guild members.

We whiled away two delightful days visiting the exhibits at the Craftsman's Fair. We listened to plaintive hill tunes coaxed from hand-made dulcimer strings with a goose-quill plectrum. We watched Lila Marshall's nimble fingers roll corn shucks into clever dolls and fairy-tale animals. An old Tennessee gentleman worked pliable white-oak splints into a stout woven chair seat for a gout rocker, that unique low, back-less chair seat with rockers on it that is used in front of an ordinary rocking chair so that the gout-stricken are not obliged to forgo the pleasures of rocking while elevating the painful limb.

We watched the artisans of many crafts turn native materials of the Appalachians into beautiful and useful objects. Basket weavers, blacksmiths, potters, broom makers, candle makers, silversmiths, wood-carvers, block printers, rug makers, needleworkers and handweavers—all were there. My husband easily made his contacts with craftsmen who could supply the Country Store with items we needed.

Our business trip seemed more like a holiday. We tasted sourwood honey and tried to see the queen bee in a glass hive seething with honey-bees. We watched the folk dances of the mountain people done to the rhythm beat of their clog shoes. We bought block-printed notepaper, a hand-dipped candle, a wren house, a whimmydiddle and a Della Robbia wreath made of dried mountain flowers, pods, cones and nuts.

Outdoors we stood by a split-rail enclosure while a woman in pioneer costume, tending a steaming black iron kettle hung from a log tripod over a hot wood fire, dipped hanks of wool yarn into dye made of sassafras chips. The spicy scent of sassafras mingled with the smell of wood smoke was magnificent. The fragrance was truly memory-making. All around us, draped over the split-rail fence, were bright wool skeins the "pioneer" woman had colored with natural dyes made from fruits, roots, and barks gathered on the mountainsides. The dye names were entrancing—sumac, pokeberry, dog hobble, acorn, pecan, rhododendron, goldenrod, smartweed, broom sedge, cocklebur, butternut, black walnut, sourwood, hickory, maple. The skeins were a botanical record in name and in color of trees and plants growing on the Smoky Mountains, which towered over the village of Gatlinburg in a flame of autumn color.

One exhibit inside the auditorium compelled me to return again and again. A serenely beautiful lady from the deep South sat before a handsome, timeworn footwheel spinning a delicate thread of flax. In the midst of this impressive gathering of skilled artisans what she did represented to me the very epitome of artistic expression. She did her simple task, woman's work since Eve's daughters spun on the rock, wearing a chic dress she had sewn from linsey-woolsey fabric she had woven from the linen and wool threads she spun on her old spinning wheel.

The sound of the wheel whirring and the tones of her soft southern

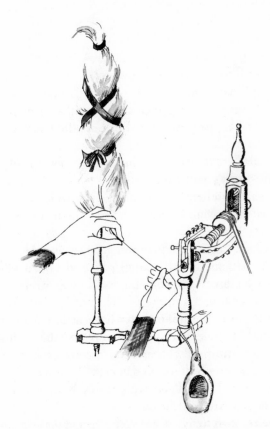

A simple task, woman's work since Eve's daughters spun on the rock.

voice, while she chatted with us who watched as she pulled flax from the distaff and spun it, reminded me of another day when I had fallen under the spell of a spinning wheel.

I remembered that day of lost days when a riot of goldenrods bloomed in Grandpa's meadows, when unwieldy carders scraped across tufts of greasy fleece, when fragrant pots bubbled and steamed on a cast-iron kitchen range, when images of snow-covered sledding hills stretched endlessly across my imagination, when the golden thread of a child's fascination was first spun out of sheep's wool.

The whirling wheel I watched in Gatlinburg became my Lorelei. I was re-enchanted.

I found my husband talking to the skilled whittlers from the John C. Campbell Folk School.

"I'm going to buy a spinning wheel," I announced.

THE SERENDIPITY

On the way home every *Antiques* sign flagged us to a stop. We poked around in dusty sheds, garage shops, tumbledown barns, in junk shop after *Junque Shoppe*. But time after time the triumph of discovery eluded us.

"Not for sale," said one. The handsome foot wheel in his shop window was the shop's hallmark.

"Oh, no," said another, "I couldn't sell the wool wheel. I inherited it from my great-aunt Maude. I just keep it here because it's too big for the house."

"I'm sorry," she said. "That spinning wheel is sold."

"I'll have to be honest with you all," he said. "That wheel's busted so's it's no good for anything 'cept for looks. You won't spin no yarn on that."

But, oh, the thrill of thinking you have at last made the find. In the rear of a poorly lighted store you have spotted the outline of a spinning wheel on a horizon of clutter. You are trapped for the moment in casual conversation with the shop owner, who won't leave your elbow although he has just said, "I'll let you folks browse 'round by yourselves. Holler if you need me."

You examine with feigned interest the cut-glass goblets, a brass spittoon, a "Bennington" pitcher, a Seth Thomas mantel clock, and rows of "gen-u-ine" carnival glass he points out for your attention.

"That's very nice," you comment politely, careful not to show more than lukewarm interest.

While he spiels, you glance widely around the room, as if taking a general look at the array of collectibles crowding the shop, but really for the sake of one more secret glance at the spinning wheel you are dying to see.

Finally the proprietor tires of touting his wares and returns to the job of scraping paint off a table in a corner of the store. You make your way, roundabout and not too rapidly, toward the rear of the store where you see the dim outline of the spinning wheel.

Then comes the disappointment of seeing that *your spinning wheel* is little more than a wheel and a bundle of splinters.

Frustration and despair crush your hopes, but only for the moment. You will continue the search at the next *Antiques* sign along the highway.

So you buy the blue spongeware bowl you found while working your way over to the dark corner that promised, for ten suspense-filled minutes, the treasure you covet. Your husband adds the brass spittoon to his collection of cuspidors. Each of the children chooses an Indian arrowhead.

You leave the antique shop wishing that the wonderful spinning wheel you saw through the cobwebs had been more than a mirage, but you're happy as can be with the blue spongeware bowl you found in its place, a discovery you would not have made had you not looked for the spinning wheel.

And so on to the next antique shop, to the next *Junque Shoppe,* to the next dusty shed overflowing with discarded relics of the past.

All winter, no matter where I looked, I could not find the spinning wheel I wanted. The search itself led to scores of happy discoveries that gave me pleasure. My collections grew. Wooden butter molds, amber canning jars, toleware, antique cooking utensils, Uhl pottery, old cooky cutters, hardy hand-sewn quilts and sturdy handwoven coverlets turned up wherever I looked for the spinning wheel. For the Country Store I found numerous old canisters and containers bearing obsolete advertisements, a pot-belly stove, the liar's bench, coffee bins, spool cabinets, Putnam Dye boxes, a cracker barrel, old store scales. Our collection of general store memorabilia and old store fixtures grew to impressive proportions.

Soon I felt truly gifted with serendipity, like the Three Princes of Serendip who in their travels were always discovering, by chance or sagacity, things they did not seek. Though I enjoyed my serendipity, I was frustrated not to be able to find the spinning wheel I wanted so much.

It was not until spring, when my husband and I were out antiquing, looking for old meat blocks and pie cupboards, that my serendipity worked in reverse. In the loft of a drafty barn near St. Meinrad, Indiana, I finally found my spinning wheel. I was looking for a tin-door safe, not a rarity in that German community, and there it was—a great, dark wheel mounted on a slanted three-legged bench, complete with spindle and pulley.

Mr. Troesch, the jaunty, fat Dutchman who operates the Steam Engine Barn & Antiques, where he does business in the loft on Sundays after church, was very reluctant to part with the spinning wheel.

"Dat's de best gottdam vheel I efer had, by golly." He shook his head negatively. "By dam, voman, I hate like hell to part vith 'er. Dammit, vhy you haf to ask me to sell dat vheel? Hell, I don't know vhen I'll efer find anoder. Gottdam!"

Mr. Troesch followed us around the loft while we looked at pie cupboards, still sputtering about the spinning wheel. I was not at all sure his tirade meant he was going to sell "dat gottdam vheel." I was afraid he was working up to a not-for-sale decision. There were items around the barn that I had tried to buy at different times, and I had learned that when Mr. Troesch said, "I von't sell," he meant it.

To get his mind off the subject of the gottdam vheel and to make the visit to "Mr. Trash's" complete, I let myself be taken, for the umpteenth time, by Mr. Troesch's practical jokery. I pulled out the cardboard carton pushed halfway under a table and looked inside. A snake lay coiled in the box—I knew it was only plaster of paris, but I shrieked dutifully.

Mr. Troesch shook with laughter. "I got dat in dere for nosy vimmen like you."

"Serfs her right, eh?" Mr. Troesch gave my husband an elbow in the ribs. "Hey, you vanta hear a good yoke?"

I left them at once and hurried off to finish looking around the loft, then down the wide stairs, where one of Mr. Troesch's many handprinted adages reminded me: *Vatch Steps I Aint Inshured.*

The time came to settle up. Mr. Troesch unsnapped the bib of his blue "oferhalls" and took out his palm-size record book and a short stub of a pencil. He wrote on the back fender of one of his gaily painted steam engines which are parked in the shed beneath the barn loft.

"Tree safes," he said. I checked my list and noted the price, though it was hardly necessary. Mr. Troesch's memory is infallible. He never forgets a quoted price. None of his merchandise bears a price tag, although many pieces are tagged with admonitions and adages, some of them ribald.

"One zink, one butcher's block, fife trunks, one box canning chars," he counted. "Dat vhat you got?"

"All except the spinning wheel." I braced myself. "You *are* going to sell me that spinning wheel, aren't you?"

"Gottdam, voman!" Mr. Troesch let loose with another volley of protest. "Vhy you put me on de spot like dis? I sell you dat vheel, den I ain't got none. Gottdam, you tell me vhere I can get anoder?"

"Now, Mr. Troesch," I teased, "you'll have another one the next time we come up here. I bet you've got a spare back there in the smokehouse right now."

"Gottdam, no, I ain't."

Mr. Troesch often kept choice and duplicate items hidden in the smokehouse. "Gottdam vimmen drife me crazy if I don't," he told us once.

Mr. Troesch fussed and cussed, but he didn't actually say he wouldn't sell the spinning wheel, so I listened to his scolding like a disobedient child. This was a game of cat and mouse.

When I figured he had surely had enough fun teasing the prey, I stopped cajoling, mustered up my best woebegone look and let my shoulders droop. I heaved a big sigh and laid my checkbook on the fender next to his little record book.

"Okay," I said, "how much?"

Mr. Troesch consulted his record book.

"Vell, gottdam. Okay. Tree safes, one zink, butcher block, fife trunks, one box chars—*and spinning vheel*. You can haf it! Gottdam! Add 'er up!"

The spinning wheel was mine.

The next time we went back to Mr. Troesch's barn there was another big wool wheel in the loft. He had added several small wheels as well, including a Pennsylvania Dutch square wheel, which he agreed to sell to me without a single word of protest.

"I see you found another big wheel, after all," I commented.

"Yah!" The crafty old Dutchman laughed. "But de best vun *you* got." He wagged a finger at me. "You been goot customer, dat's vhy. Odervise I still haf dat gottdam vheel."

There are moments, especially when it throws off the driving band one time after another while I am spinning, that I wish Mr. Troesch still had his "gottdam vheel." But old spinning wheels, like old spinsters, tend to be contrary at times. This tendency, as I see it, elevates the antique spinning wheel from the class of inanimate objects and gives it personality, however unpredictable.

Mr. Troesch's old wheel, then, is entitled to its stubborn habits and iodiosyncrasies because it is at least two hundred years old. I accept it. I am reconciled to approaching it with a special attitude that borders on the mystical.

When the spindle fills quickly with fine spun yarn, as if I were Rumpelstiltskin himself—"Whirr, whirr, whirr! Three times round and the bobbin was full"—I am bedazzled into thinking that I am finally mistress of Mr. Troesch's cantankerous old spinning wheel.

Then, before I can say "My name is Rumpelstiltskin," the spinning wheel takes a stubborn notion to throw its driving band. No amount of coaxing, crying or cussing ("Gottdam vheel!") will make it behave. The fine thread is reduced to straw on the spindle. Like the miller's daughter, I say, "I don't understand the business," and abandon Mr. Troesch's old wheel for a more tractable (and less interesting) spinning wheel.

Still, the yarn I spin on Mr. Troesch's gottdam vheel is like golden thread spun from straw. The stubborn old wheel is my serendipity, found where a tin-door pie safe should have been, mine because of a happy accident of discovery.

It still protests my ownership by throwing its driving band, echoing Mr. Troesch's voluble but halfhearted protests, but I am its mistress because I found it by chance and made it mine by sagacious bargaining.

And I wouldn't trade it for a Rumpelstiltskin.

The pleasures of *finding* your wheel add immeasurably to the joy of spinning, to the charm of your wheel. And you should be charmed by your wheel, even beyond the point of reason, if you are to enjoy spinning with it to the fullest measure.

So be aware. Explore the drafty barn loft or dusty attic. Ferret out the spinning wheel whose past is dimmed with cobwebs. Welcome the hard bargain made for the coveted prize. Cherish the gift of serendipity. Enjoy the crusty old proprietors of out-of-the-way antique shops. Attend the country auction and taste a subtle, reckless excitement while coolly bidding for the spinning wheel you are determined to have, regardless of price.

Get off the beaten track. Bravely approach a likely looking mountain cabin in the Ozarks or the Appalachians and inquire. Heed the bidding of signs along the highway and follow bumpy back roads into unfamiliar territory.

If you find your spinning wheel by such methods, by chance or by sagacity, you will find much, much more.

You might remember, as I do, a road such as the one in Virginia that led me up the side of a mountain toward *Peckinpaugh's Antiques— 5 Miles.* How long five miles seem to be when there are no houses along the road until finally you see a tumbledown log cabin where a tangle of wild sweet peas bloom on the road bank, spilling over onto the narrow road's edge. Stop at the curve to better see the pink tangle of sweet peas and to peer at the log cabin, wondering, "Is *this* it?"

Get out of the car to look at the name on the mailbox, which is half covered by fragrant vining sweet peas. Suddenly you are surrounded by dozens of swirling butterflies, a flock of sparkling silver-spangled fritillaries that are sipping nectar at the bower of sweet peas. It is an other-worldly moment. You remember it.

On up the mountain to the very top, where you find *Peckinpaugh's Antiques,* a breathtaking view and a charming Saxony spinning wheel. You are eight hundred miles from home and the car is loaded, but you buy it, dismantle the wheel and crowd it into the back seat.

The Peckinpaughs find a rope in the barn, disturbing a flock of nervous guinea hens, which explode around your head and feet with feathers flying. An early Windsor chair and a small pine table, found by serendipity on the mountaintop in Virginia, are lashed onto the top of the car.

Now there is room for only one boy in the back seat of the sports coupe, so the other small boy moves up to the front to share a seat. It is less than cozy for two in a bucket seat during an eight-hundred-mile trip home, but fortunately you are blessed with a trio of good-humored men who are dyed-in-the-wool antique hunters.

You feel like migrating Okies, driving into the motor hotel in Lexington, Kentucky, with a Windsor chair and a pine table on the luggage rack, its cover flapping in the wind, and a spinning wheel in the back seat with rearranged luggage stuffed around everywhere. But you endure the jokes of filling-station attendants and tighten up the ropes that hold the cargo in place.

Once at home the mountaintop discoveries look better than ever. You are no less pleased than Great-Great-Grandmother Marshall when her household goods came safely over the mountains from Virginia through the Cumberland Gap. It was worth it.

The new-found Saxony spinning wheel is set before the hearth and soon its whirring, thumping music fills the room. The spindle flies around and around and you make a thread that one day will stretch out as long as a road up a lonely Virginia mountainside. When you spin you remember swirling, spangled butterflies and fragrant wild sweet peas and speckled guinea hens and the Peckinpaughs and eight hundred miles in a bucket-seat-for-two. You have a mountaintop feeling whenever you spin on the Saxony wheel.

You understand why the Saxony wheel has a special aura of its own, an aura that comes of all the incidental pleasures of the quest compounded by the thrill of *finding* what is sought.

BUYING AN ANTIQUE SPINNING WHEEL

Suppose you find an antique spinning wheel you fancy—what then? To encourage chance in the hunt is wise, and fun besides. But once the spinning wheel is found, you cannot trust Lady Luck to clinch the bargain in your favor. You must know how to tell if the wheel is workable (unlikely) or repairable. You should know what repairs the wheel needs so that you can judge whether or not it can be restored to working condition. You should have an idea of the wheel's value or you run the risk of being fleeced in the exchange.

Few old spinning wheels are found with all their original parts, so watch for ill-fitting replacements that have been substituted for missing pieces. You may discover parts of the wheel in ridiculous places; the wheel itself may be mounted on the wrong end of the bench or a flax distaff might be attached to a wool wheel. Study the diagrams of the different types of spinning wheels shown in this book and learn which parts belong where.

Seldom is the spinning wheel equipped with the driving band, made of ordinary staging cord, which drives the spindle when the wheel is turned. Without this simple cord you cannot tell if the wheel works at all. Carry a suitable piece of string with you when you are looking for your spinning wheel. You can tie it on quite easily and try the wheel before you buy it.

If you haven't a band, at least pump the treadle or turn the wheel to test its action. The wheel may run smoothly and easily or seem to require only a dab of Vaseline on the axle. If the wheel is quite wobbly or out of line, you had better look more closely or have your handyman look it over before you buy. A wobble may be cured with a piece of leather, but it could also mean a warped wheel, which is a bad buy.

Watch out for badly worn grooves in the bobbin pulleys. They may be replaced or the grooves can be built up, but you are much closer to being able to spin when your wheel needs only small repairs or adjustments. If you buy a spinning wheel with a missing spindle or flyer, you may search for some time to find a replacement that will fit your wheel.

How much should you pay for a spinning wheel? At an antique shop you will pay the current going price for your wheel. This price varies with the condition of the wheel and the availability of spinning wheels in the area. To determine the current price of spinning wheels in your area, consult your librarian. Current prices of antiques are published in various magazines and books. Shop around and look at price tags; compare local prices with listed values. Ask other spinning-wheel owners what they paid for their wheels. Then decide what you are willing to pay. Your dealer may expect to bargain or he may have only one price. Let your intuition and his reputation guide you.

When you are buying a spinning wheel out of someone's attic, you encounter one of two situations. One owner places no value whatever on the spinning wheel, sentimental or monetary, and will take practically anything you offer for the "useless" old wheel. In this case you may have the spinning wheel at your price and just let your sense of fairness and the circumstances of the owner be your guide. The other owner greatly overestimates its worth because someone told him he owned a valuable antique spinning wheel, and the first price you offer, no matter how much, will never be enough. My advice is to forget it. Do not attempt to continue bargaining if your offer insults this owner. You can seldom buy from the owner who has an inflated sense of value, and you can never make a happy bargain with him either.

The price you pay for a spinning wheel at an auction depends upon both chance and sagacity, or, in other words, on the weather and

You have acquired the best working wheel you can find at an auction or from someone's attic.

your competition. If someone else wants the spinning wheel you want, it is a contest of wills, with the more determined of the bidders paying the top price or more. At small country auctions, which are not well advertised, you may have fewer antique dealers, pickers and collectors to bid against. When there are several auctions in the area on the same day, you have a better chance to buy at a good price, because there are only so many auction buffs and they won't all be at the auction you attend. Cold weather and rain help your cause too, as fewer women and more farmers will brave the elements to attend the auction, and farmers are not interested in spinning wheels.

If you are really gifted with serendipity, you may find an auction at which you are the only one interested in the spinning wheel. No one else will bid against you for fear of getting stuck with the closing bid. I once bought a wool wheel for five dollars in those circumstances and it gave me a very wicked thrill. What luck!

Since you will make a better bargain at an auction or when buying a spinning wheel out of someone's attic, you will not mind paying to have the wheel repaired. But if you are paying the top price for a spinning wheel in an antique shop, you should be more discerning.

Suppose you have acquired the best-working wheel you can find at an auction, at an antique shop or from someone's attic. You may find yourself at a standstill. Where do you find a tradesman who lists repair of spinning wheels among his services? Certainly not in the Yellow Pages of the telephone directory.

Ask the antique dealer for the names of persons who repair and restore antiques. Or inquire at the local museum; the curator may be able to help you find a craftsman. Or write a spinners' or weavers' guild near your home. Someone who shares your interest will know a craftsman who will repair your wheel.

Replacement of missing parts may send you on still another search, or you might have your missing part custom-made by a local craftsman. See "Spinning Wheels and Accessories," page 169, for addresses of firms that carry replacement parts for spinning wheels and repair broken wheels.

Buying a New Spinning Wheel

Suppose you fail to find an old, experienced spinning wheel to suit your fancy. What then?

You may be surprised to know that brand-new spinning wheels are being made today. At present most of those available in the United States are imported from other countries where need for warm clothing, or textile artistry, or availability of flax and wool has never allowed the craft of handspinning to be as nearly abandoned as it was in this country during the past century. Now, as the revival of interest in handspinning as a craft gains momentum, more home-produced spinning wheels are becoming available. See "Helpful Information" to learn where to find them.

Some of the new American-made spinning wheels are faithful copies of Colonial wheels. They are well-finished, handsome and unusual pieces of furniture for the home as well as efficient spinning devices. Others are purely functional in design. Also available are spinning attachments designed to operate in conjunction with a sewing machine, either electric or treadle.

A variety of styles are available. Last year in Canada I bought a new parlor-type wheel for wool spinning. From Norway you might acquire a new Saxony-type spinning wheel with the typical level Scandinavian bench; from Yugoslavia, a small parlor flax wheel with distaff; or a chair-type wheel made in Canada which is very functional in design.

When you buy a new spinning wheel there is no delay while you look for replacement parts, no search for a handyman to build up a worn pulley groove. There is no cleanup or refinishing to do. The tension screw stays where you put it and the driving band does not fly off because the wheel is slightly out of kilter. New wheels do not act contrary, as old, time-worn spinning wheels sometimes do, although I expect each to develop its own tendencies as time goes by. When there is a precise bit of spinning to do or when I simply lack the patience to cope with an old wheel's idiosyncrasies I spin on one of the new wheels.

New spinning wheels have no bad habits—but neither do they have the aura of romance that surrounds an old spinning wheel resurrected by you from a cobwebby past.

CHAPTER THREE

Four Housewives
Learn to Spin

My quest for a spinning wheel led us over half of the United States. It began in Gatlinburg, led us through Pennsylvania, up a Virginia mountainside, down to the Ozarks, up across Tennessee and Kentucky, and finally to a barn beside a country road in the southern Indiana hills, where I found my first spinning wheel. The search lured me to auctions and into attics, enticed me to country sales, obsessed me with antique shops, craft festivals, restorations and museums and gave me grit enough to gain entry wherever I lacked it.

It was a rewarding search, starred with serendipity. Our home today is brimful of treasures found those days when I looked for a spinning wheel but found something else instead, which I value today. All about I see reminders of a pleasant day's outing, of a musty attic, of a rainy day when I huddled in a leaky, three-sided shed waiting for the auctioneer to offer the item I wanted to bid on.

When finding a spinning wheel ceased to be the major obstacle between me and the golden thread I felt compelled to spin, another problem took its place. All the while I collected spinning equipment I failed

33

to meet a single person who could actually spin thread. There was no one who could teach me to spin on one of my wheels. Nor could I find anyone who could remedy the various ills of my ailing wheels so that I might try, at least, to teach myself by trial and error.

When the subject was spinning wheels my standard inquiry of likely looking persons was, "Can you spin?"

"My mother always told how she remembered her folks a-making yarn for their clothing," one old-timer told me, "but she didn't know how 'twas done herself. I don't neither."

Or, with a shrug of the shoulder, "Far's I know, this wheel ain't been used since my granny used it. I cain't learn you how."

Memoirs and recollections by the score whetted my desire to spin all the more, but apparently there was not a single living person left this side of the Appalachians who could actually spin on a spinning wheel.

All the grandmothers, aunts and mothers who spun the thread fine as silk were dead and gone. Only tattered shreds of their efforts and rich memories of their accomplishments were left to the heirs. None had seen the necessity of passing on her skill to the next generation. The need for handspinning no longer existed, and the absence of need means death of a craft.

In the short span of one or two generations practical knowledge of spinning had passed from the realm of a commonplace, everyday chore to the category of folk art and craft. Only a few devotees, and those far between, fanned life back into the dying craft by spinning for spinning's sake.

One day, about a year after I had found my first spinning wheel in Mr. Troesch's barn, I learned of one of those persons dedicated to preserving crafts in this area. A small item in a local newspaper announced an exhibition in a neighboring town of handcrafted items made by members of the Lincoln Hills Arts and Crafts Association. The highlight of the show was to be a demonstration of spinning by Brother Kim of St. Meinrad Archabbey.

Surprise and delight! Someone in the vicinity was spinning, after all.

I drove to Lamar, Indiana, and arrived at the school gymnasium, where the program was being held, during the dinner hour. As fate would have it, I missed seeing Brother Kim and the spinning demonstration, but there on the platform were baskets of fleece, carders, and spinning wheels, their spindles filled with spun yarn. Spinning was alive in southern Indiana, drawing its first breath instead of the last.

I drank a cup of sassafras tea, a February tradition in southern Indiana, and learned from the hostess that Brother Kim offered free spinning instruction to all interested members of the Lincoln Hills Arts and Crafts Association, which he had helped to organize. I was eligible to join the association as I, too, lived in Lincoln country, but the classes were held at night in a building at the monastery in St. Meinrad, Indiana. It was out of the question for me to drive a round trip of one-hundred miles to St. Meinrad by myself, at night, in late winter when the hilly, curvy roads were often slick, to take lessons in spinning from a monk at the abbey. Then, too, the monastery itself was awesome, built like an impenetrable fortress of huge rosy-tan blocks of St. Meinrad sandstone, high on a hill above the Germanic village, where local speech is still strongly laced with the language of the fatherland. Of monks I was even more in awe. I simply did not have enough gumption to undertake the trip or continue the project alone.

Now I needed someone to join forces with me, to share the involvement and the long trip to St. Meinrad Archabbey.

Late winter is not the traditional time of beginnings, but, rather, of endings. My friends and relatives, who I hoped would find my project intriguing, were deeply entrenched in the ruts of winter schedules. Thursday nights were reserved for bowling, the P.T.A., bridge, basketball, and the like.

Discouraged, I shelved the idea of learning to spin at the monastery for the time being and pitched into a much-needed session of "spring" housecleaning, that housewifely madness that besets me yearly during Lent.

The clutter of spinning paraphernalia was crowding us out of our home. Spinning wheels graced every corner of the house. As décor they were overdone.

"It's rather like living in a museum, isn't it?" I quipped one day when my husband was picking his way across the bedroom to the closet where he kept his sweaters.

"All you need is a sign," he commented. "*Junque Shoppe.*"

In its uselessness my spinning-wheel collection was losing something of its glow. My husband was tired of tripping over them, and they were terrible dust-catchers. We decided to remove the overflow to the Country Store, where a little dust on a tacky spinning wheel would add favorably to the old-time atmosphere.

The small wheels were placed on a high ledge above the shelves of merchandise, in the company of cigar-store Indians, old bottles, clocks, carpet beaters, washboards, tobacco tins and sundry antiquities.

"No price tags!" I warned.

Some of the contributions I had made earlier to those upper shelves in the interest of "atmosphere" were gone forever, because the good proprietor is conditioned, à la Pavlov, to ring a cash register upon hearing a generous cash offer.

"Don't worry," he said. "I'll keep them, if only so no other poor guy will have to stumble over them."

So my favorite wool wheel was hoisted high and suspended above the thick hand-hewn beams supporting the second-floor balcony of the store. It was handsome there, displayed against the rose-brick wall and safely out of my husband's path.

On its lofty perch the great dark silhouette became a true conversation piece. It drew comments daily from admirers below—a round of small talk, a flight of nostalgia, and frequent offers to buy.

Pledged to refuse the latter, the proprietor often tempered the finality of "Not for sale" with a chatty explanation that I would use that one for wool spinning if or when I found someone to teach me how.

"I have exactly the opposite problem," said one dark-eyed, smiling, enthusiastic woman who wanted to buy my wool wheel. "I have the teacher but no spinning wheel."

Mary Jane Steele wanted to learn to spin, and *at once*. She was restoring an old Rappite home in New Harmony, Indiana, a nearby town originally founded as a communal society by followers of George Rapp, and it was scheduled to open for the public on the day of the Golden Raintree Festival early in June. In the Epple Haus she had arranged displays of handspun, handloomed household items of the Rappites, and she planned to have spinning wheels and weaving looms in operation to demonstrate these once-common domestic crafts.

When our paths met, under Mr. Troesch's cantankerous old wheel, there was precious little time left for Mary Jane to complete her plan. It was now early spring, with fields greening up and forsythia showing buds.

"Look," Mary Jane said, "I'll take you to my teacher if you'll take a turn spinning in the Epple Haus this summer."

I agreed eagerly, and our alliance began. Within one week Mary Jane, with characteristic efficiency, bought three fine old Kentucky spinning wheels (as well as a giant loom), rounded up two more spinning companions, and arranged for our spinning lessons. The teacher was, of course, Brother Kim at St. Meinrad Archabbey.

Our companions were Marion Warweg, Newburgh artist and weaver, who wanted handspun threads for her looms, and Marge Danner, organizer of the Arts and Crafts Fair held on New Harmony's village green during the Golden Raintree Festival. Although we were barely more than strangers from neighboring towns, we four housewives shared a warm camaraderie from the beginning. Our personal reasons for undertaking this unique venture were varied, but we soon discovered that we all felt a common obligation to help preserve the ancient craft of spinning for contemporary women.

Four housewives wedged into a station wagon with a conglomeration of spinning wheels, bound for a monastery to learn to spin yarn by hand in this age of push buttons, synthetics, and automation present something of an anachronism. But, four strong, we were brimming with determination and purposefulness.

We drove through the gateway of the St. Meinrad Archabbey as the great bell in the church tolled seven.

"Right on time," Mary Jane said. "Now, let's see, it's the building next to the quarry offices—so that must be it."

We followed the curving drive to the back of the large building built of rosy-tan sandstone, which the Benedictine monks quarry from the nearby hills. We parked in front of two enormous sliding doors.

"This looks like some kind of a garage," Marge said. "Are you sure we're in the right place?"

"I don't see anyone around, either," Marion observed. "Are you positive we have the right night?"

"Positive." Mary Jane said. "Right night, right place. But it does look like an empty garage." She opened the car door. "Wait here, gals," she said. "I'll have a look in this building."

She tried the small wooden door next to the two larger ones. It was open. Just as she stepped into the semidarkness of the building the Archabbey church bell began to toll again. This time it called the devout to evening worship.

"Of course!" Marge exclaimed. "That explains it. Everyone here must be in church."

Moments later Mary Jane reappeared. We were right. The lower portion of the building was a garage, and *almost* all the monastics were in church or had retired to the seclusion of their quarters for the evening.

Brother Kim's enthusiasm for spinning wheels was obvious.

Three brothers in charge of the arts and crafts workshops were beginning classes in the upstairs rooms over the garage.

Each carrying a spinning wheel, we threaded our way, none too
quietly, through the clutter of the shadowy garage. Hearing us, Brother
Kim, a pleasant young man wearing a dark-blue denim apron over his
black habit, greeted us from the top of the stairway.

Brother Kim's enthusiasm for our spinning wheels was obvious; he
especially admired Marion's Bavarian one-hundred-fifty-year-old parlor
wheel. Within minutes he was rummaging around in drawers and
closets for string, bits of leather, oil, and various tools he needed to put
our wheels in order.

Though Brother Kim's workshop was actually a spacious room,
its very low ceiling, which ended just above the doors, the several large
looms, spinning wheels, and a plethora of spinning and weaving accouterments in the typical disarray of the craftsman's workshop, combined to give the room a feeling of the traditional garret studio. Except
for Brother Kim's black garb and the regular chiming of the Archabbey
church bell on the quarter hour, the workshop might have been located
anywhere.

Wall hangings of contemporary design, woven on vertical looms
with vegetable-dyed threads, hung on the walls and from the conven-
ient ceilings. Skeins of handspun wool, labeled according to the natural
dye material used to color them, hung from nails driven into a central
ceiling beam. A dye pot bubbled over the burner of a gas stove against
the wall. Quilts, rag rugs, a coverlet, hooked rugs, interesting scraps
and samples of weaving and knitting were at hand in every quarter
of the room. Weavings-in-progress were in several of the looms and a
hooking frame held a half-finished hooked rug. The variety of design
and technique attested that these objects were the expressions of many
hands.

There were only two other women attending the workshop that
evening; one was warping a loom for weaving and the other was weaving a length of woolen suiting fabric. There were no other spinners in
the workshop.

While we explored his workshop Brother Kim quickly made the
simplest adjustments to our spinning wheels. The more complicated
repairs he promised to complete before we returned the next week.

Then we gathered around the handsome spinning wheels that
Brother Kim had found in the monastery, stored away and forgotten
since the days when yarn was spun for monastery use. As he explained

the parts of the wheels and their workings, some of the mysteries of our own wheels vanished. Brother Kim helped me oil my ocher-painted Saxony wheel and I was ready to try spinning as he showed me how.

For all of us the first evening of spinning was a series of attempts and failures. We experienced all the beginner's difficulties. The yarn was too thick and lumpy to pass through the orifice or too much twist formed in the yarn. The fibers were not drawn out enough or so much that the yarn broke. The treadling was uneven or the wheel suddenly reversed in direction and ran backward. When all else worked smoothly, the end of the yarn or even the unspun rolag flew into the orifice and wound around the bobbin with such speed that we were amazed to find our fingers empty.

But after Brother Kim's simple directions each of us at last understood what we were attempting to do. Brother Kim assured us, as my grandmother had once assured me years before, that we would all get the knack of it with a bit of practice.

The next day at home I moved my Saxony wheel in front of the hearth, where women have always spun and where a warming fire always crackles in the grate, and passed the peaceful afternoon in pursuit of the elusive knack of spinning. The perfection I had seen in Grandmother's spinning and in Brother Kim's I felt within myself, very near expression at my fingertips. I had only to free the quick movements I visualized, the lyrical motions I remembered, to spin out the continuous, soft thread that began somewhere inside me.

As I practiced, mastering one phase after another, I could feel the synchrony of the spinning wheel and my motions, the smooth perfection of the spun thread slipping through my fingers, and that synchrony gave a wild exhilaration to the peaceful afternoon.

The exhilarated feeling was reinforced as each bobbin filled with spun yarn. This was a special joy I felt, a basic satisfaction that was to deepen and grow as I followed the golden thread stretching out from its beginnings in Grandfather's goldenrod-filled meadows to a never-ending point just beyond my grasp.

CHAPTER FOUR

Woolgathering

Baa, baa, black sheep,
　　Have you any wool?
Yes, sir, yes, sir,
　　Three bags full;
One for my master,
　　And one for my dame,
And one for the little boy
　　Who lives down the lane.

—Old Nursery Rhyme

It was after supper on an unseasonably cool May evening when Mrs. Davis called.

"The sheepshearers are here," she said. "I thought maybe you and your boys would like to come over to watch."

We grabbed sweaters and hurried to the car. The tide of excitement ran high. We had expected the call from Mrs. Davis for a month or more. She had promised to arrange for me to buy a fleece from the people who came to their farm every spring to shear the sheep. The sheepshearers were given the fleeces in exchange for the service of shearing.

I had no fleece to spin on my spinning wheel. The supply given to me by Brother Kim had run out. During the winter my friends and I had spun the fleece of a Merino sheep grown in Ohio and four precious pounds of wool that had been shipped via air freight from California. Now it was spring and time for sheep to be shorn, but none of us had learned where to buy fleece near home.

My sons and I had driven up and down country roads with an

eye out for sheep grazing in fields. Few farmers in Warrick County raise sheep, and we did not know who or where they were. Our search for the pastoral scene took us over a cobweb of backroads, an enchanting odyssey that netted us no wool. The sheep we found grazing in pastures were already shorn. We were too late, it seemed.

Everywhere that I inquired, "Have you any wool?" I received the same perplexing reply. "We never keep any fleece," the farmers said. "The fellow who shears the sheep takes the wool for his trouble. I think it all goes to the Wool Pool."

My friend Mary Jane was having the same problem.

"Marilyn," she moaned, "no matter where I go, the Wool Pool has been there before me. The farmers around New Harmony don't bother with the fleece. They raise sheep for mutton or to keep the weeds down. No one seems to know what happens to the fleece after the man shears the sheep. No one seems to know who the man is who shears the sheep. He just appears every spring. If we want homespun wool from home-grown sheep," Mary Jane advised, "we'd better get our own sheep."

But before rushing out to buy a lamb of my own I decided to call the county agricultural agent.

The Wool Pool, I learned, is within a price-support program of the United States Department of Agriculture. The farmer takes his wool to the stockyard, is paid the going price for the fleece, and the fleece goes into the "pool." The farmer then takes a receipt for his wool crop to the Agriculture Stabilization and Conservation Service Office. The ASCS records the farmer's wool crop, files the necessary papers with the USDA, and the farmer is subsequently paid a government subsidy.

"Let me send you a list of sheep owners who live near Newburgh," the county agent offered. "This cool weather has slowed down the shearing. You should be able to find a farmer who hasn't shorn his sheep yet."

I was surprised to find on the list he sent me the name of a family on Epworth Road, one road over from Grimm Road, where we live. The farm buildings and pastures are secluded behind trees and we had not seen their sheep though we drive by the Davis farm daily.

I talked with Mrs. Davis and learned, happily, that their sheep had not yet been sheared. She thought it might be possible to keep one fleece for my spinning wheel from sinking into the depths of the Wool Pool.

Now, this evening, we were invited to the Davis farm to watch

Old wool shears.

the shearing of the sheep. We would deal directly with "the fellow who shears the sheep and takes the wool."

It was a short drive to the Davis' small farm. We turned in the lane and pulled up at the side of the white frame house. An Irish setter rushed up to the car to bark at us. Children appeared at both corners of the house. They stared timidly at us until we stepped out of the car. Then the largest child, a girl, ran forward.

"They're around back." The words were barely said before she turned and ran behind the house.

Left to find our own way, we followed the brick path around the house and walked across the grassy backyard to a small pen not far from the back door of the house.

Inside the sheep pen a man and a woman, twin figures clad in white coveralls, prepared for the sheepshearing. The man, a young, husky fellow with sandy hair and the ruddy, weathered skin that marks the farmer at any age, spread a large sheet of white canvas on the grass next to the fence. The woman was almost as big as the man. She wore sturdy oxfords, and a red bandanna was knotted around her neck. The sharp wind brought color to her cheeks and tousled her close-cropped red hair. In spite of her mannish attire and stature, she looked quite feminine and marvelously healthy. She moved purposefully around the sheep pen, unwinding long black cords attached to two enormous clippers with edges of sharp, comblike teeth.

Mr. Davis was shepherding his small flock of thick-fleeced Hampshire sheep into the pen. When the handsome dark-faced sheep reached the gate at the end of the lane leading from the barn they balked at entering the pen. It was as if the sheep knew something was up, and at the gate a special dread overwhelmed them. They bleated piteously and milled around but refused to go through the gate. Mr. Davis prodded them gently with a stout stick and shouted, "Hu-ey, hu-ey!"

At the sound of shouts the Irish setter appeared and began barking at the sheep through the fence. Finally the sheep bolted through the gate and ran across the pen to the far corner, where they huddled together. They took shelter under branches of a wild cherry tree drooping over the fence from the other side of the enclosure, and there they waited for their doom, baa-ing forlornly and pushing nervously into the center of the flock.

Mrs. Davis came out of the house carrying a small, clean paint brush and a tin can filled with pine tar. She greeted us.

"How do you like this weather?" she asked. It was the easy country way of starting conversation when people do not know each other, the first step toward that common ground beyond the weather.

The boys shivered and hugged their shoulders to demonstrate their discomfort.

"Isn't it too cold to cut off their warm coats tonight?" Jimmy asked.

Mrs. Davis said they'd keep the sheep closed in the warm barn at night until the weather changed. She explained that sheep are usually shorn of the heavy winter growth of wool in early spring, when warm weather first sets in. They had not been shorn as early as usual this year because the weather had turned cool, and stayed cool, after an earlier, short-lived spell of hot weather. For once the sheepshearers were not rushed to finish the season of shearing because the animals were suffering under a hot May sun in heavy wool coats.

Mrs. Davis carried the tar can inside the sheep pen and set it on top of a fence post.

New clippers with oil can.

The lady sheepshearer finished unwinding the long electrical cords of the clippers. She plugged them into the socket of a heavy black extension cord that trailed across the grass into the sheep pen from an outbuilding nearby. Then she left the enclosure and went to a truck parked outside the fence. She removed an enormous white sack from the truck and hung it over the wire fence. This bag would receive the fleeces shorn from the sheep. Then she walked around the rear of the truck and removed from the truck bed a large oil can with a long narrow spout. She knelt on the edge of the canvas sheet and oiled the clippers. When she had finished she set the oil can on the ground outside the small gate at the front of the pen. She latched the gate and began pulling on a pair of white cuffed gloves with leather fingers and palms.

"I guess I'm ready," she announced to the men, who stood talking together at the edge of the white canvas sheet. "Are you?"

By way of answer both men started walking with slow careful steps toward the corner of the pen where the sheep huddled. They reached the edge of the flock before the jittery sheep scattered. Both men lunged, arms outstretched, toward a frightened yearling ewe with a lush coat of virgin fleece. The luckless sheep was caught by neck and legs and pulled, pushed, and dragged to the front of the pen, where the woman waited, hands on hips.

The big man straddled the captive sheep. Releasing his hold on the animal's jaws and neck, he grasped both forelegs and lifted until the ewe was forced upright on its hind legs, its woolly back held tight against his stomach. Then with one foot he pushed the young sheep's hind legs out from under her body, and the bewildered ewe sat down on her haunches on the white canvas. Before the sheep could scramble to her feet again the man rolled her over on her side and pinned her down to the canvas with one knee across her shoulder and ribs.

I felt sympathy for the helpless, frightened ewe. She lay quietly under the man's knee, but her dark eyes were wild with fear. The manhandling of the timid animal was not in harmony with the idyllic sheepshearing I had envisioned. I had pictured gentle, willing sheep lying comfortably or standing quietly while being sheared to "give" us wool from their backs for our warmth and comfort. I remembered the gentle attitude of the peasants shearing their lamb in Millet's painting "The Shearing" and the lamb's meek submission. I'd expected the shearing to compare more with the grooming of a loved pet, to be a pleasurable experience for both shearer and shorn—not this sheep rodeo.

I looked at my sons' faces. Having no sentimental or preconceived notions of a sheepshearing, they were heartily enjoying the disposition of the sheep to the canvas.

"Hey!" Jimmy was taking it in with wide eyes. "That's neat!"

"It's just like wrestling," Bobby said. "Look at that *neat* hold."

. The woman flipped the switch on the big clipper. A harsh buzzing resounded and the cutting teeth oscillated rapidly.

The man took the noisy clipper from his wife and plunged the scissoring blades into the deep fleece on the ewe's rear. He undercut the thick wool with sure smooth strokes and began to roll back a blanket of lush cream-colored fleece, laying bare pink skin on the sheep's hindquarters.

Now Mr. Davis went again to the corner of the pen and selected the next animal to be shorn, a dark-faced sheep with a creamy coat of thick, curly fleece. The farmer caught her firmly by the neck and steered her to the front of the pen. The woman swung a leg over the ewe's back, grasped its forelegs, flipped the ewe to the canvas and pinned it down with her knee.

It was apparent that the lady could hold her own when it came to handling sheep. She dispatched the sheep to the canvas as neatly as her husband had.

She took the clipper that Mr. Davis handed her and cut a swath of wool around the ewe's rear. The air reverberated with the buzzing

Lady shearing a sheep.

of the powerful clippers. We watched, fascinated, as the blankets of wool rolled back and the sheep were left naked.

The animals lay quietly and made only halfhearted attempts to get up. If a sheep raised its head or kicked a leg the shearer subdued the animal with a free hand and pushed down more firmly with the knee, and the clipper buzzed on.

Occasionally a spot of red appeared on the bare skin of a ewe where clippers nicked the skin when the animal moved or where the clipper blades ran up against a protrusion of skin or bone hidden by deep, curly fleece. Then Mr. Davis stepped up and daubed tar on the wound with the paint brush. The tar prevents green flies from sitting on the wound and safeguards against maggot infestation.

The shearing took on the feeling of a race. There was a spirit of good-natured competition between the sheepshearers, even though the man had the advantage of a head start. There was a steady flow of banter between them.

"Aren't you finished yet?" he kidded.

"I'm catching up with you," she came back. "Better hurry!"

"Well, you ought to finish first." The man kept the ball rolling. "My critter's bigger than yours."

"You started first." She laughed. "Anyway, mine's livelier."

The atmosphere was easier now. We relaxed and began to savor the experience. The pair inside the sheep pen were more relaxed, too, now that the task was under way and going well.

When one side of a sheep had been shorn clean the shearers rolled the sheep over on the other side and continued without a break. In only a few minutes the man had cut the last bit of fleece free from the sheep's neck. The fleece came off all in one piece. The man tossed it to one side, stepped to his feet and released the shorn sheep.

The naked ewe scrambled to her feet and ran back to the flock, an ugly, unnatural-looking animal that bore little resemblance to the charming, cuddlesome sheep that had entered the pen.

From then on, Mr. Davis had all he could do bringing up sheep, keeping fleeces moved out of the way, and daubing the spreading red spots with tar. The man and woman kept up the fast pace they had begun. The light banter between them continued too, even though everyone in the sheep pen was out of breath and weary by the time the last sheep had run off to the security of the spreading branches in the corner.

The last sheep ran away before Mr. Davis had daubed its wounds

with tar. He went into the corner to finish his task and the woman
leaned againt a fence post to rest. The man squatted on his heels and
fanned his face with his small-billed cap. He wiped sweat from his
forehead with a crumpled red bandanna like the one his wife wore
knotted at her neck.

"If the missus gets any better at this haircutting"—he winked at
Bobby and Jimmy—"I'm going to sit under the shade tree and boss."

The missus started winding up the long black cords attached to
the clippers.

"If the *boss* is sitting under the shade tree when I'm done with my
share," she said to the grinning boys, "he may have to walk home."

The boss jumped up quickly, in mock haste, and spread out the
fleeces for me to make my selection. I chose the first shearing from
the young yearling ewe. It would spin softer yarn than the fleeces of
sheep that had been shorn before.

I touched the long soft fibers and remembered her dark, wild eyes.
Even now there was an aura about the pile of fleece lying there on the
white canvas, something of the sound of sheep baa-ing, the smell of tar,
the chill of the wind we had felt on our faces as we stood outside the
sheep pen.

"I want this one," I said.

The man rolled up the remaining fleeces, tied them and dropped
them down into the big white woolsack, which, when held up, was
longer than he was tall. He carried the woolsack to the back of the
truck and tossed it over the tailgate into the truck bed.

He walked to the front of the truck and touched the horn. At the
signal the children we had seen briefly when we drove up an hour
before appeared immediately from the house. Two of them jumped into
the truck bed and fell down laughing on the softness of the white
woolsack. The third child, the one who had told us where to find
the sheep pen, went back inside the house.

Mr. Davis came out of the sheep pen, still carrying the tar can, and
the two men exchanged thanks. The sheepshearers climbed into the
cab of the truck and drove off with their laughing children and the
sackful of fleece in the back of the truck.

"Well, now," Mr. Davis said, turning to me. "Let's see what we
have here."

He rolled the fleece shorn from the yearling ewe and put it into a
burlap bag. He hooked a brass hand scale into the top of the sack and
held the sack off the ground.

"Weighs nine pounds, eight ounces," he said. "Price of wool is sixty cents a pound. I make that to be five-forty, plus twenty-five cents for the sack, unless you want to bring it back sometime when you go by. That all right with you?"

I wrote out the check. We said goodbye to the Davises and thanked them for letting us watch the sheepshearing.

Jimmy hoisted the sack of fleece to his shoulder and we walked down the brick path to the car. Jimmy put the sack of wool in the back seat of the car and we drove down the lane away from the secluded little farm. At once an odor of lanolin and tar and stables and burlap filled the car.

"Phew!" Bobby's nose wrinkled.

"Stinks, doesn't it?" Jimmy socked the soft sack of fleece.

Bobby rolled down a window. "Well, Mom," he said, "*now* you have some fleece."

"Yes," I said. "It's very special fleece too."

"And I bet the yarn you'll spin from it will be the best yarn you've ever spun."

"I hope so."

"I liked that little sheep the best of all," Bobby said. "Maybe you could make me something out of her fleece."

"I will," I promised. "Think about what you'd like."

"I already know," Bobby said. "I want a long striped scarf with fringe on the ends, long enough to wrap around and hang down my back."

I thought of a bright-yellow woolly cap with a long tail that flies in the wind as the sled skims down a long snowy hill and never, never reaches the bottom.

"You shall have it," I vowed, "before the first snow flies."

Breeds of Sheep and Grades of Wool

The fine-wooled Spanish Merino sheep were developed from sheep brought to Spain by the Romans under Claudius. Although the breed was closely guarded to protect Spanish wool interests (the penalty was death for spiriting Merino out of Spain), Merino eventually reached France in 1786, and Louis XVI kept them in the national sheepfold and developed from them the Rambouillet sheep. These two fine-wool

BREEDS OF SHEEP AND GRADES OF WOOL

	BREED	U.S. BLOOD GRADE	SPINNING COUNT	AVERAGE YEARLY STAPLE	FOR HANDSPINNING
FINE-WOOL BREEDS	American Merino	Fine	64s to 80s	2¾"	Creamy color; heavy grease; soft yarn; the finest fleece for woolen spinning.
	Delaine Merino	Fine	64s to 80s	2½ to 3"	
	Rambouillet	Fine and Fine medium	62s to 70s	2¼ to 3"	
CROSSBREED-WOOL BREEDS	Corriedale	¼ and ½	50s to 60s	Over 4"	Long, silky fiber; good for beginners.
	Columbia	Low ¼ and ¼	50s to 60s	3½ to 5"	
	Panama	⅜ and ¼	50s to 60s	3 to 4"	
	Romeldale	½	58s to 60s	3½ to 4"	
	Targhee	½	58s to 60s	3"	

	Breed		Count	Staple	Description
MEDIUM-WOOL BREEDS 	Southdown	½ and ⅜	56s to 60s	2"	Very white, fine, well-crimped fleece.
	Shropshire	⅜ and ¼	48s to 56s	2½"	Some black fibers may show in fleece; makes nice woolen yarn.
	Hampshire	⅜ and ¼	48s to 56s	2 to 2½"	
	Suffolk	⅜ and ¼	48s to 56s	2 to 2½"	Light, airy fleece; easy to spin.
	Dorset Horn	¾ and ¼	48s to 56s	3 to 4"	Very white, strong fleece.
	Cheviot	¼ and ⅜	48s to 56s	3 to 4"	Excellent to spin.
	Oxford	Low ¼ and ¼	46s to 50s	3 to 5"	Soft fleece; easy to handle.
LONG-WOOL BREEDS 	Leicester	Braid	to 48s	7 to 9"	Long, lustrous staple with wide crimp; coarse; makes good knitting worsted, tapestry yarn.
	Romney	Braid	40s to 48s	5 to 6"	
	Lincoln	Braid	36s to 46s	8 to 12"	
	Cotswold	Braid	36s to 46s	8 to 12"	

breeds, the Merino and Rambouillet, became the foundation sheep breeds for the world.

There are now about two hundred breeds of sheep in the world. Of those a dozen or so are important breeds in the United States. Commercially their wool could possibly be classified into two thousand qualities, based on diameter, length of fibers, color, crimp, and other factors.

For the handspinner such elaborate distinctions are not necessary. Simply knowing the degree of fineness of fleece and the length of fiber to expect from a certain breed of sheep are enough to help the handspinner buying fleece for her spinning wheel. The United States Department of Agriculture blood grades for wool and the commercial spinning count are most often used to make these distinctions in fineness of fiber and staple length.

The USDA blood grades for wool are based on the proportion of fine-wool blood in the breeding of sheep raised in the United States. There are seven standard blood grades of wool ranging from the finest to the coarsest fibers: Fine, ½ Blood, ⅜ Blood, ¼ Blood, Low ¼ Blood, Common, and Braid. The English system of grading by spinning count also indicates the fineness of the fiber. Spinning count refers to the number of 560-yard hanks of wool yarn it is possible to spin out of one pound of wool top.

CHAPTER FIVE

Preparing Wool Fleece
for Spinning

Although I now had a bagful of wool for my spinning wheel, I could not spin yarn for Bobby's striped scarf (*"with fringe on the ends, long enough to wrap around and hang down my back"*) until I had sorted the fleece of the yearling ewe.

SORTING THE FLEECE

I would have preferred doing the woolsorting outside in the fresh air, but three affectionate dogs and four playful cats always await my exit from the back door, so the back porch seemed the better place. First I spread a thick layer of newspapers on the porch floor. Then I slipped the bundle of fleece out of the burlap sack onto the newspaper. It was folded in thirds lengthwise, with the shorn side outside, rolled up neatly and tied several times around with paper twine.

I clipped the twine and spread the fleece out flat so that I could

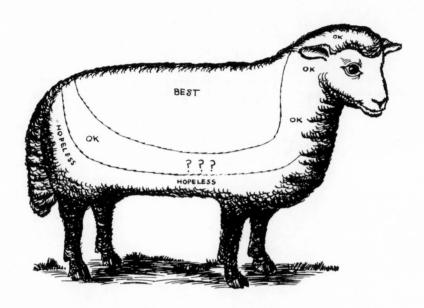

Best, O.K., Hopeless—categories that would horrify a professional woolsorter, but for my purposes they were adequate.

examine it carefully. The outer edges of the shorn fleece, which formerly covered the sheep's stomach, legs, head, neck, and rear, appeared to be the dirtiest and coarsest portions of the fleece. The central area of the fleece, from the sheep's shoulders, back and sides, was fairly clean, and the fibers were longer and finer than those from the outer edges of the fleece.

I gathered up some cardboard cartons and penciled labels on them: *Best, O.K., ??,* and *Hopeless.* These categories would horrify a professional woolsorter, but for my purposes they were adequate. I needed only to separate the dirty, unusable parts from the good wool, and the short, coarse fibers from the longer, fine ones.

First I skirted the fleece, taking off at least two inches all around the entire outer edge. Of this the dirty portions from around the tail and under the stomach of the sheep went into the *Hopeless* box to be burned later. I pulled out burrs and threw away tags and locks of wool that were badly matted or fouled with dung. I picked out the short second cuts, snips of wool left in the fleece when the shearers make a second cut to even out the shearing. All the unusable and filthy fleece went into the *Hopeless* box.

What remained of the belly wool was tender and fine but short in length. Rather than throw away anything unnecessarily—Where was my next fleece coming from?—I saved it too. The belly wool would do for dyeing samples. It went into the questionable box—??—along with wool from under the sheep's neck and the short face wool.

The coarse wool from the sheep's hind legs and haunches went into the *O.K.* box. It was harsh but strong, and too good to throw away. Into the same box went any wool that seemed to me to be on the borderline, not really nice enough for Bobby's striped scarf but worth saving. I would use the second-best wool to make heavy yarn for wall hangings.

The best wool was left now. The longest crinkly fibers from the sheep's shoulders, back and upper sides went into the box marked *Best*. This was the very special fleece from which I would spin yarn for Bobby's scarf before the first snowfall of winter.

The best wool from the yearling ewe, which was quite clean, was ready to be carded and spun into yarn just as it was, without washing. The coarser wool I planned to give a preliminary washing and dyeing in the fleece before carding and spinning into yarn for art textiles.

The wool fleece my grandmother made into yarn for my woolly cap that long-ago day was spun unwashed, or "in the grease." Newly shorn top-quality fleece of normal staple length is best spun in the grease. This is often a fragrant experience because the odor of wool is quite distinctive, but most spinners feel that fleece handles more easily when the natural lubricant, lanolin, or "yolk," is present in the wool.

Still, there are times when the only alternative is to wash the wool beforehand. The wool of an entire fleece is sometimes extremely dirty and odoriferous. If the fleece is old the natural grease may have dried and hardened. Then you will decide that the wool must be washed, or "scoured," before you work with it.

SCOURING WOOL FLEECE

Washday should be bright, breezy and sunny. Plan to wash only a small amount of fleece at one time. If the fleece contains a lot of vegetable matter and loose dirt, shake and toss it on a coarse screen to dislodge as much waste as possible before washing.

Use several containers for washing and rinsing fleece, each large enough to allow the fleece to float freely in the water. Fill the containers with soft water that is comfortably warm to the hands but not hot. There are many recommendations for higher temperatures of water for washing wool, but special reservations accompany their use. See *Other Washing Methods,* page 58, and *Handling Wool,* page 145.

Use rain water if possible. Catch some during a downpour in a rain barrel under a gutter spout or in pails, or draw it from a cistern. Well water, especially artesian, is usually hard. Tap water and spring water are hard too. Clear, running stream water or river water may be soft. If the water is not soft, use the same water softener you use for the family laundry.

Use a mild detergent for washing the fleece. Submerge the fleece in the sudsy water and squeeze it gently with the hands. Never pour the water on the wool and never churn it around in the water. Pick out trash as you squeeze the wool under the water. Never lift the wool above the water while washing it.

The water in which the wool is being washed will become extremely dirty almost at once. Squeeze out the wool and wash it again in sudsy water of the same temperature. Be very careful not to have the second water, or successive waters, either hotter or cooler than the first one. Wool cannot tolerate being subjected to sudden extremes in temperature. High heat or sudden changes of temperature of the wash water cause the fleece to mat (felting) and the wool fibers to harden. Wool can stand a high temperature or temperature changes of the water only if brought to them gradually. See *Other Washing Methods* and *Handling Wool,* pages 58 and 145.

When the wool fleece has been put through at least two sudsy waters, squeeze it out and rinse through several clear waters that are the same temperature as the water in which the wool was washed. When the rinse water is clear and the wool fleece is clean enough (dirty wool floats, clean wool sinks), squeeze out as much water as you can with your hands. If you have a wringer-type washer or a portable wringer, run the wool through the wringer to express the water. Or place the wool fleece in a mesh laundry bag and run your automatic washer through the spin cycle only.

During the Renaissance the bag containing the wet wool was tied on a stick and whirled vigorously to remove excess moisture. This was "wuzzing" in the seventeenth century, a feeble version of the centrifugal extraction employed in our automatic washers.

In washing fleece, use rain water if possible.

DRYING WOOL FLEECE

To dry the wet wool fleece, lay it out on an old window screen placed on the backs of two chairs, or contrive a similar arrangement that allows the air to circulate freely through the fleece. Set up the drying rack in a breezy place, not in full sun, and turn the wool once in a while. After the fleece has lain on the screen for a time you may find that you can gently squeeze additional moisture out of the wool.

Of course wool fleece, like wool garments, should not be dried close to a heat source or in an automatic dryer.

RETAINING LANOLIN

Washing in warm water according to the procedure above removes most of the dirt and natural grease in the wool fleece. There are times when the spinner would rather remove only the dirt from the fleece and retain the natural lanolin. Lanolin lost through washing must be replaced by enough carding and spinning oil to make the fibers easy to handle. Then, too, sweaters knitted from yarn retaining the natural grease are water-repellent and the spinner-knitter may never want to lose the lanolin in the fleece. Irish Fisherman and Aran Isle sweaters are knitted from wool that still contains the natural wool grease of the sheep's coat. While garments made of this yarn will not keep one bone dry in a downpour, they resist a moderate amount of moisture and are very warm.

When cold water is used to wash the fleece, the natural lanolin is retained. Submerge the fleece in cold water with a small amount of mild detergent in it. Allow the wool to steep in the cold water for several hours without squeezing it. Wool fibers do not open and release dirt so readily in cold water as in warm water, so allow plenty of time. Then rinse the wool thoroughly in several cold rinse waters, using a minimum of agitation, and dry in the manner described above.

My Kentucky friend who keeps sheep for her own spinning wool has the sheep dipped shortly before they are shorn. This dunking removes a great deal of the dirt in their fleece but saves the natural lanolin so that Minnie Alice can spin yarn "in the grease," as she prefers.

OTHER WASHING METHODS

You may want to try other washing methods for wool. Remember the general rules to prevent damage to the wool fibers:

Never change temperature of water suddenly.

Never subject wool to boiling temperatures.

Never pour water directly on wool.

Never agitate wool vigorously.

Never lift saturated wool above the water without support.

USING AN AUTOMATIC WASHER

My friend Virginia washes wool fleece in her automatic washer inside a strong net bag used for washing lingerie in a washing machine. She fills her top-loading washer with water that is comfortably warm to the hand (below 120° F.) and adds detergent as for the family laundry. She immerses the bag of wool in the water, then gently presses the bag by hand to dislodge the soil. She does not agitate the bag of wool with the washer. When the water is dirty she sets the washer to spin out the waste water. The bag of wool is removed, the washer filled again with sudsy water of the same temperature as the first suds, the bag of wool is returned to the water and allowed to soak for ten minutes. Again the washer spins out the soiled water. Rinsing is accomplished in the same manner, with the water temperature remaining constant and the bag of wool never allowed to be under the stream of water entering the washer.

HAND-WASHING METHODS

A spinner I met in Canada at a spinning seminar gave me her formula for scouring wool. She said: "Put the dirty wool in 120-degree-Fahrenheit water to which you have added 1 tablespoon of salt and 2 tablespoons of Tide detergent. Let it get cold. Then lift out the wool without agitation. Now repeat the process *without the salt* and let it stand overnight. If it still needs washing, put it in tepid suds. If not, start rinsing in tepid water. Then hang it on the line and let it blow." This formula refers to the skeins of wool, but can be used with fleece, except that fleece must be dried on a rack.

Greentree Ranch in Colorado recommends a prerinse with a little salt or soap in the water to remove the bulk of the dirt. Then immerse the fleece in warm water with your favorite laundry soap added. Place the container on the stove and bring the temperature of the water up to "very hot," which can be from "hand hot" of about 120° F. to 180° F. (The United States Department of Agriculture recommends 150° F.) Allow the fleece to steep for about 10 minutes, then remove from the heat and leave the fleece in the water until it cools. Rinse the fleece several times in water of the same temperature as that from which it was removed.

VARIATIONS

Directions I received from a Canadian firm suggested the addition of one-fourth cup of coal oil (kerosene) to the last rinse water. This makes the wool fluffy, and, surprisingly, the odor of kerosene does not cling to the wool.

A friend from Brown County, Indiana, always uses salt in the water she uses to wash wool fleece or newly spun yarn. Her washing formula is one teaspoon detergent to the gallon of warm water and one-half teaspoon salt.

Cold-water detergents may be used with success for scouring wool. Woolite, a cold-water soap made especially for wool, is excellent, though expensive for large quantities, but it removes the natural grease in spite of the cold water—a result you may or may not desire.

SOAP OR DETERGENT?

Any soap residue left in the wool after scouring will interfere with proper dyeing of skeins or fleece. Detergents do not leave an alkaline residue and are preferable if you intend to dye your wool. If the wool is to be left its natural color, use either soap or detergent.

Long-time spinners swear by their own tried-and-true scouring methods and washing preparations. The beginner will experiment a bit before deciding which suits her best of all.

"CRICK WATER SURELY MAKES THE WOOL NICE."

If you have a clear running brook on your property, you might take your fleece there, as I do, and wash it in the stream. This method of washing fleece is as old as the craft of spinning itself. Taking the wool to the water is a lot easier than bringing the water to the wool. You need not bother with washtubs, and the stream carries the soiled water away. Fish will not be endangered if you do not use a detergent to wash the wool.

I decided to try washing my wool fleece in a running brook, pioneer style, after I became acquainted with a wizened old lady of ninety who visited me at the Newburgh Country Store. She saw a feature article in the Evansville *Courier* about my spinning wheels and it stirred in her a poignant nostalgia for the past. She had a strong hankering to see a spinning wheel again and her granddaughter drove her to Newburgh so that she might satisfy her desire.

The spinning wheels that appeared in the newspaper photograph were in the front window of the store being used as props for the window display.

The old lady touched the Saxony spinning wheel. "My, my," she said. "I once span many a thread on a wheel like that one. I'd surely love to see a spinning wheel a-working again."

"That one works," I said. "Would you like to spin on it?"

"Goodness, no," she demurred. "I couldn't do it any more. Lands, its been nigh seventy years since I span a hank of yarn."

"We'll take it out of the window," I said. "You can have a go at it if you like."

The proprietor lifted the spinning wheel out of the window. I moved the checkerboard out of the way and he set the spinning wheel in the clearing in front of the potbelly stove. I gathered up hand carders and fetched a basket of wool fleece.

The old lady gave the wheel a few tentative turns while we made ready, but when I placed a small chair in front of the wheel for her to sit on, she lost the courage to learn if she could still spin.

"My hands are old and stiff," she said. "I'm afraid I can't do it any more. Besides, I wouldn't want to put your wheel out of working order."

"Go ahead," I urged her.

"No," she said. "I'll just sit here while you spin, if you will be so kind."

Instead of sitting on a chair nearby, she squatted down on her heels right out in the middle of the floor beside my spinning wheel, an unbelievable position for a person of her age and quite the most un-orthodox position of sitting for anyone older than the age of two.

She maintained her dignity, oblivious of the stares of customers shopping in the store, and refused a chair the proprietor offered, saying, "I find this very comfortable, thank you."

So while the ancient lady squatted, yogilike, on the floor beside me, I spun "sentimental yarn" for her, as my grandmother had once spun yarn to please me.

While I spun she spoke of the old days in the mountains of eastern Kentucky where she "took a school" when she was a young woman.

"My schoolhouse was tolerable cold in winter," she said, "and we dressed warm. I knitted all my woolen clothing—stockings, mittens, sweaters. All the folks thereabouts kept sheep so as to have the wool for spinning.

"There was a clear-running branch in the woods below my cabin," she went on. "I always carried my fleece down the hill and washed it in the crick until it was pure white. That was the old way. Folks wouldn't do it that way now, but crick water surely makes the wool nice."

Aside from the convenience and soft water, the pleasures of a morning spent at a brook's edge washing wool fleece—the sun's rays

Dry wool in open air when possible.

sparkling on the water and warming your shoulders as you kneel on a hard stone, hands tingling in cold water and senses tingling with awareness of all that is around you—can only compound your enjoyment of the yarn you spin from the fleece.

And, I agree—"Crick water surely makes the wool nice."

RECONDITIONING SCOURED FLEECE

When the natural grease has been washed away from wool fleece it can still be spun but will feel dry and harsh to the touch. Without natural lanolin in the fibers the staples do not open out as nicely during teasing, and fibers are more difficult to twist together while spinning the continuous strand. Consequently it is best to replace the natural wool grease with another oil before trying to spin scoured fleece.

Which oil to use is an arguable subject among spinners—animal, vegetable, or mineral? The oil should be water-soluble of course, so that it will wash out easily. Any grease left in the yarn will keep dye from taking. Some oils become rancid after a time and others have distinctive odors that offend the sensitive nose. Experiment to find your own preference.

Mineral oil is a good spinning and carding oil because it is water-soluble, does not become rancid, and has no odor. It should be diluted, 3 parts oil to 1 part water, and beaten to an emulsion. Spray the wool with the emulsion while tossing the fleece, wrap it in an old woolen cloth, and let it lie overnight before teasing and carding.

Brother Kim recommends olive oil, a vegetable oil, to replace the lost lanolin. Merely shake a good quantity of olive oil over the scoured fleece while tossing the fleece. Leave the fleece for a day or two to give the oil time to spread through the wool. Turn the fleece occasionally while it is soaking up the oil. Later, while spinning the carded fleece, dip your fingers into olive oil if it seems necessary. Remember to wash the olive oil out of the spun yarn before it turns rancid.

Another solution used to replace natural grease lost in scouring wool fleece is made by adding 4 ounces of washing soda dissolved in a half gallon of water to enough neat's-foot oil to form a milky emulsion. Sprinkle this solution over the wool fleece and use it to lubricate the fingers while spinning.

In the Southern Highlands, not so long ago either, scoured fleece was well greased with lard to make it spin easier. More than likely, bacon drippings or renderings from ham rinds would be used before clean, white lard, a home product not to be wasted.

Another olden-days custom, that of sitting at the fireside while spinning and carding, not only chased away chills but was beneficial to the wool. Warmth from the fire opened up the wool fibers and softened the natural grease in them. The carders worked better too when warmed.

When you add oil to wool you intend to spin the next day, adapt this old custom to your procedure. Wrap the oiled fleece in a warmed cloth and keep it in a cozy place until you begin to card and spin—why not near the fireplace? (But, mind you—not too near; oiled wool makes good tinder.)

> Cross-patch,
> Draw the latch,
> Sit by the fire and spin;
> Take a cup,
> And drink it up,
> Then call your neighbors in.
>
> —Mother Goose Rhyme

STORING WOOL FLEECE

Naturally you cannot leave wool fleece resting in a container that you do not want stained with oil. The oil in the wool, either the natural lanolin or an oil you have added, will seep into other fabrics or materials touching the wool.

Greasy wool fleece should not be stored in a closed airtight container, because it is a combustible material. Always store unwashed wool fleece in a dry place in an open or porous container, such as a basket or burlap sack, so that air will circulate through it. Do not store unwashed wool fleece in an attic or in a place where it might become overheated, increasing the danger of spontaneous combustion.

If wool fleece is to be kept for any length of time before spinning, it must be scoured. The natural grease in the wool becomes hard with age and the wool fibers become weakened. When wool fleece has been washed it may be kept for much longer periods without loss of quality. One woman keeps washed wool in enormous glass jars with screw-top lids which she gets from her grocer who receives pickles in them. She has kept several jars of wool like this for more than five years and it is as fresh as ever.

It is a good idea to add mothballs to all wool fleece or spun yarn that must be stored for any length of time lest our wool, like Penelope's, "fill Ithaca full of moths."

CARDING WOOL FLEECE

Most wool must be carded before it is spun into yarn. Carding the fleece—combing seeds and burrs out of the wool while straightening the fibers—was what I did to help my grandmother that long-ago afternoon when our goldenrod yarn was spun.

Wool carders, or cards, are wooden paddles onto which carding cloth made of leather inset with bent wire hooks is mounted. My grandmother called them "wool combs," which is what they are.

The words "card," "carders," and "carding" are derived from the French cardère, which means "teasel." Teasels are the prickly seed heads of a wild plant, Dipsacaceae, which were used in earlier times to comb wool fibers smooth before spinning them into yarn. A teasel head makes

Fuller's teasel,
prickly seed heads
once used to card wool.

a primitive but satisfactory stopgap wool carder when nothing else is available.

ANTIQUE WOOL CARDERS

Grandmother used hand carders like those on page 68 to card fleece. I have several pairs of century-old carders, like Grandmother's, which I bought at country auctions and in antique shops. These carders are in very good condition and I use them (with care!) to card the fleece I spin. My favorite pair of antique carders are Number 10's, which, according to the description printed on the wooden paddle, are designated for combing cotton bolls. They do an excellent job of preparing fine wool fleece for spinning and I prefer them to new wool carders.

Good antique carders are hard to find. Most old carders found in antique shops or at auctions have teeth missing and the leather through which the teeth are attached may be rotten and crumbly. Nevertheless I urge you to carry on the search until you find an old pair of wool cards in good condition. Then pamper them, but use them. Using the old carders, when you have found them at last, perhaps unexpectedly, gives another dimension to the joy of spinning, made sharper by the pleasures of the search itself.

My friend Marion, still looking for a satisfactory pair of old carders, has found that by using only her fingertips she can tease the wool and straighten the fibers sufficiently to spin beautiful yarn. Sometimes she lays the lock of fleece on her lap and combs it with an ordinary hair comb. Most of us would find Marion's method of straightening the wool fibers laborious and time-consuming, but Marion is an artist who finds aesthetic delight in the whole process of spinning from carefully teasing and arranging the fibers by hand to spinning the yarn on her one-hundred-fifty-year-old parlor spinning wheel from Bavaria.

NEW WOOL CARDERS

New wool carders are manufactured today and can be bought from companies and suppliers in the United States and Canada. See "Where to Buy Supplies" for a list of sources.

SIZE OF CARDERS

It is a good idea to have several sizes of carders for carding wool fleece. The coarser carders, such as Number 8, work best on coarse fleece, and the yarn spun will be heavier. For the fine wools and a finer yarn a Number 10 carder, with teeth set closer together, serves the purpose better. Some spinners card the fleece through a coarse carder first, then through successively finer ones.

The fleeces from different breeds of sheep vary in length of staple and fineness of fiber. The size carder used should be chosen accordingly.

CARE OF CARDERS

The carders should not be loaded too heavily, nor should coarse fleece be pulled through a fine-toothed carder. Always use the same carders for the right hand and the left hand. Do not pull one carder heavily and flatly across the other; rather, use a light brushing motion with heavier pressure at the top of the right-hand carder.

Grandmother always put her carders away between times with a lock of greasy fleece between the teeth. The lanolin in the wool kept the leather from drying out and preserved it. In wintertime she never used the carders cold, but gave them a chance to warm up after bringing them down from the unheated attic room where she kept her weaving loom and the magical spinning wheel that once had spun out a golden promise for a small girl.

How to Card Fleece with Hand Carders

Fleece should be teased before carding. Teasing, or picking, spreads and fluffs the fibers in the lock of fleece, which may be somewhat matted together, without pulling it completely apart. Seeds and trash in the fleece fall out or can be picked out during teasing.

Hold the lock of fleece in the left hand, cut-tip up. Use the fingers of the right hand to gently pull the lock of fleece, a bit at a time, from the left hand to the right hand with a side-to-side, gathering motion. This loosens the fibers without pulling the lock apart. Do not loosen the lock of fleece by pulling it from the tip, or cut end.

Teasing fleece.

Wool fibers for carding with hand carders should not be much longer than the width of the carders for woolen spinning. Fibers of 2- to 4-inch staple are usually spun by the woolen method from a rolag of carded fleece, while much longer fibers require combing instead of or in addition to carding. Long fibers are spun by the worsted method.

Distribute a small portion of teased fleece evenly across the teeth of the left-hand carder. The cut end of the lock of fleece should

Loading carder with fleece.

be at the top of the carder. Do not put too much fleece on the carder; use only a small lock of teased wool. Always use the same carder for the left hand so that the teeth are not damaged by improper meshing. Mark carders "Left" and "Right" to avoid confusion.

Starting position for carding.

Hold the left carder in the left hand, with its handle pointed away from your body. The back of the left carder may rest on your knee, with the teeth facing upward. The fleece lies laterally across the teeth of the carder.

Hold the right carder in the right hand, with the teeth facing down.

Place the right carder over the left carder, which contains the wool. Pull the right carder downward, brushing gently across the left carder while pulling the left carder slightly upward in the opposite direction. See below. The larger brushing motion is made with the carder in the right hand, the left carder being almost stationary. Use a light brushing motion with slightly more pressure on the top edge of the right carder. Do not drag the right carder flatly or heavily across the bottom carder. Not only does the flat drag require more muscle but it damages the carding teeth and the wool fiber as well.

Pull the carders in opposite directions several times. This procedure straightens the wool fibers and makes them all lie in one direction. During the combing, dirt and trash fall out and some of the fleece transfers to the teeth of the right carder. It must be transferred back to the left carder before the carding can be completed.

To transfer all the fleece back to the left carder, turn the right carder so that the handle points away from the body, in the same position and direction as that of the left carder. Place both carders, teeth in the same position, facing each other, but with the bottom edge of the top carder (the right one) at the top of the teeth of the left carder as

Downward sweeping motion of carder.

Transferring fleece back to left carder.

shown above. With one downward sweep from the bottom of the right carder across the left carder, lay the fleece back on the teeth of the left carder.

Turn the right carder back to the starting position and repeat the brushing process. Again transfer the carded fleece back to the left carder.

Rolling the rolag off of the carder.

Repeat several times until the fleece is well combed, with all the fibers lying straight across the teeth of the carders, and all of the trash and vegetable matter has fallen out.

Now that the fleece is carded and back on the left carder, it is ready to be rolled up into a rolag.

Beginning at the bottom of the left carder, cards in carding position, push the combed fleece up from the bottom teeth of the left carder with the top edge of the right carder. Some people reverse the right carder and roll up the rolag with the top edge of the back side of the carder, but it makes no difference. The fleece will roll up to the top of the left carder and can be removed with the fingers.

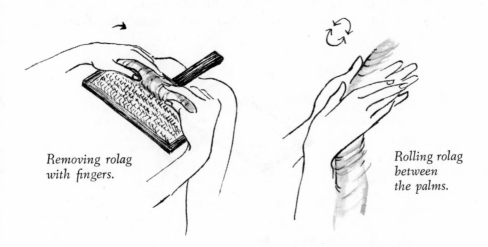

Removing rolag with fingers.

Rolling rolag between the palms.

Sometimes the rolag is placed on the back of the card and patted into a smoother shape, or it may be rolled lightly between the palms.

Lay the rolag of carded fleece aside. It should be about the size of one's middle finger. It is ready to spin.

Prepare a basektful of rolags before beginning to spin. Carding is an enjoyable task in itself, but it becomes an annoying interruption that destroys the rhythm of spinning if you must stop often to replenish the supply of rolags, which spin all too quickly onto the spindle.

Or find a companionable child to sit beside your spinning wheel who will card fleece as you spin. You may add still another intangible quality to the yarn you spin together by sharing the gentle rhythms of spinning and carding.

CARDING LONG-STAPLE FLEECE

Longwools of 4-inch staple, or longer, are spun by the worsted method, for which carding is done in a slightly different manner than for the shorter wool fibers. The latter are usually spun by the woolen method but can be spun by both woolen and worsted methods.

Long-staple wool fleece does not lend itself to hand carding as well as the shorter fibers. If the long fibers must be carded on hand carders, the rolag is rolled across the width of the card from one side to the other, rather than from the bottom of the carder to the top as for woolen spinning. This arranges the wool fibers in a roll with all the fibers parallel to each other, as they must be for worsted spinning. The shorter fibers among the longer ones can be removed during combing and saved for later use so that only the longer ones remain in the cards when finished.

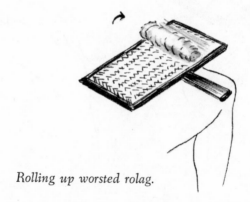

Rolling up worsted rolag.

Long-staple wool fleece can be carded on the carding machine too. Carded batts, prepared in any of the ways described, are ready for worsted spinning.

Another way to comb long-staple fleece is to hackle it through a single hand card used only for this purpose or through a metal-toothed dog comb. Comb it like flax, on all sides, pulling a lock of wool through the teeth of the implement several times until the fibers lie parallel to each other. Short fibers that remain in the comb, the noils, should be saved to card in with shorter staple wools for woolen spinning. The long fibers that are left in the hand are called tops, and only these are spun for the best worsted yarn.

Pulling long-staple fleece through dog comb.

Longwools in good condition can also be spun directly from the hand without carding, after careful teasing. The long, silky fibers draw out naturally from a lock of long-staple wool.

USING A WOOL-CARDING MACHINE

While carding is a pleasant pastime for the unhurried, it soon turns to drudgery if a great bulk of fleece must be carded. A small carding machine is the answer. When one uses this, several pounds of wool may be carded in an hour if necessary.

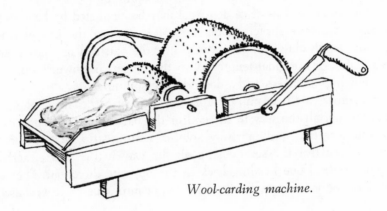

Wool-carding machine.

The machine consists of two revolving drums, one large and one small, which are turned by a hand crank. The carding drums are covered with steel combs set in leather, similar to the carding cloth on hand cards. Teased wool is fed under the smaller drum, and, after a few easy turns of the crank, the wool fibers are arranged, parallel to each other, in a neatly carded batt of wool fibers on the larger drum. Dirt and trash fall below the machine.

As the large drum fills with carded fibers a smaller quantity of wool collects on the smaller drum, which turns against the larger one. This can be removed with a knitting needle from time to time and added to the fibers on the large drum, or it can be saved to recard later for special purposes.

When the wool on the large drum seems well carded, take a knitting needle and pry up the batt of wool along the width of the drum where the ends of the carding cloth join. Lift the carded wool off the drum.

The directions accompanying my wool-carding machine suggest cutting through the batt with scissors when it is removed from the drum, but I found this unsatisfactory. Prying off the batt leaves it with a better edge for joining, albeit uneven.

Sometimes the batt of carded wool is put through the machine a second time for more thorough carding.

There are several ways to prepare the carded batt for spinning. Lay the batt in the lap and pull long, narrow strips of wool off the side of the batt as needed, spinning them by the worsted method. Draw out each strip during spinning and join a new length of carded wool from the batt to the preceding one when it is used up. The disadvantage to spinning from narrow strips just as they come from the batt is that there are frequent joinings and interruptions to spinning.

Or the entire batt of carded wool may be elongated by hand before spinning is begun, stretching out a small section of the batt at a time with the hands close together. With care, the batt can be drawn out to several times its original length. With the longer, narrower strip, much less drawing out needs to be done during spinning.

Another way is to pull off a narrow strip of carded wool along one side, but not all the way to the end of the batt, then turn back in the opposite direction, pulling away another narrow strip next to the first one. Do not tear the second strip all the way to the end either, and begin the third one heading back in the opposite direction. The strips you have pulled away will remain in one continuous piece because the

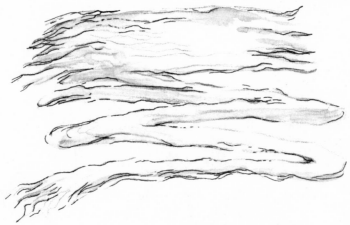

Zig-zagging the wool batt

ends of the strips are still joined. Continue pulling away the strips, zig-zag fashion, across the batt.

Spinning Methods
Used with Machine-Carded Wool

Yarn spun from batts prepared in any of the described ways is spun by the worsted method, since the fibers are arranged parallel to each other. Remember: Tighten the tension to wind the yarn on faster and use a long draw. If there are two grooves in the spindle pulley, put the driving band in the shallow groove (larger-diameter pulley) to form the least twist.

For woolen spinning from batts of carded wool, recard narrow strips lightly with hand carders and make rolags. Arrange the wool on the carders as you would uncarded wool. Since the fibers are already straightened and cleaned of trash by the carding machine, this is light work. Spin the rolag with a loose tension and use a short draw with the hands close together. If there are two grooves on the spindle pulley, slip the driving band into the deeper groove (smaller-diameter pulley) to twist the yarn firmly.

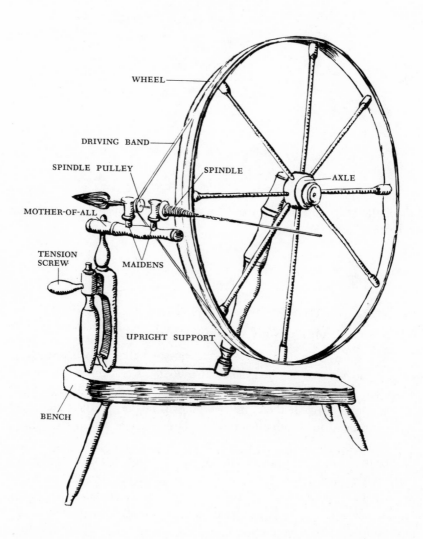

WHEEL

DRIVING BAND

SPINDLE PULLEY

SPINDLE

MOTHER-OF-ALL

AXLE

TENSION
SCREW

MAIDENS

UPRIGHT SUPPORT

BENCH

*Wool wheel, also known as "walking wheel," "long wheel," "great wheel"
and "high wheel."*

CHAPTER SIX

Spinning Yarn
on a Wool Wheel

The great, dark spinning wheel I bought from Mr. Troesch is called, most simply, a wool wheel because it spins only wool fleece. Only occasionally, when methinks it doth protest my ownership *too much*, do I honor it with the name it was called by Mr. Troesch— "Gottdam vheel!"

In the old days the wool wheel was aptly called the "walking wheel" because the spinner walks back and forth beside it to spin. She steps back to draw out the fleece over the tip of the spindle, then forward to wind the spun yarn onto the spindle. One hand turns the huge wheel while the other hand holds the sliver of fleece. Irish colonists called this spinning wheel the "long wheel," to Scots it was the "muckle wheel," Welsh families remember it as the "great wheel" of Wales, and English ladies spun their fleece on the "high wheel" or "Jersey wheel." Spinners of the Southern Appalachian Highlands still know the wool wheel as the high wheel, the flax wheel as the low wheel.

Whatever the name, the wool wheel, as I prefer to call it, is easily recognized. The basic style does not vary. A large hand-turned wheel mounted on the lower end of a long bench, either three- or four-legged, turns a simple spindle on the other end of the bench.

The wool wheel is primitive in design as compared with the more sophisticated castle and Saxony spinning wheels, which did not come into use until centuries after the wool wheel. The wool wheel replaced the hand spindle, the first spinning device, which was used to spin the threads of the unbelievably fine and enduring cloth of ancient Egypt—and before. We can use all these spinning devices to spin fine thread and yarn today, just as they were used on the banks of the Nile, in straw-thatched Irish cottages, and in the sitting room of the manor house on a tidewater plantation in old Virginia.

To spin yarn on the wool wheel the spinner must execute an intricate, rhythmic pattern of stepping backward, then forward, stop and go, "turn the wheel fast and turn the wheel slow," while holding the sliver of fleece to the front of the spindle, then to the back, twisting and winding the fibers until the yarn is spun. The wool wheel requires of the spinner skill, patience, and endurance.

The wool wheel is indeed a walking wheel. Weary spinsters, who aptly named it, walked mile after mile during an energetic day's spinning. Twenty miles before the wheel in one day was not unusual for a spinster in Colonial times. To spin enough yarn for even the simplest garment meant a long journey on foot, a hundred miles walked before the wheel, to produce enough warp and woof for one day's weaving. Handspun and handwoven coverlets and household linens represent incalculable hours of effort.

Fortunately the hardy homespun coverlets are still available to those who seek them, and sometimes, by accidental discovery, to those who seek something else. Five old coverlets I found when I was looking for my spinning wheels I owe to my serendipity—Walls of Jericho, Chariot Wheels, Lee's Surrender, Hickory Leaf, and Rose of Sharon.

My enjoyment of these sturdy coverlets, woven of handspun yarns dyed in madder and indigo and hickory bark, adds joy to spinning on the old wool wheel I found in Mr. Troesch's barn. Just such a wheel spun the yarn for my handwoven coverlets a century ago.

Now I slowly put by skein after skein of soft new yarn spun on my cantankerous old wool wheel and try to understand again the mysteries of weavers' drafts for those charming "kiverlets" that were the pride of mountain looms. But, no use—my mind boggles. The weavers' draft is a crossword puzzle with no words; the great old loom, an anagram of numbered pieces knocked apart and piled in a corner of the garage.

Remind me to get some mothballs, will you?

The Wool Wheel and Its Parts

The wool wheel is the spinning wheel in its simplest form. The spindle is similar to the primitive hand spindle except that it operates in a horizontal position instead of vertically and is rotated by the great wheel rather than by hand.

Wool wheels were brought to this country by colonists from Britain where they came into use in the fourteenth century. They were probably introduced to Britain from Holland, which was a great textile country during medieval times. It is thought that India was the home of the first spinning wheels, which date from very early times. Primitive wheels, forerunners of the wool wheel as we know it today, were used in Japan and China eons ago, with the spinner sitting or kneeling on the floor beside the wheel.

The large wheel that turns the simple spindle of the wool wheel is connected to the spindle by a driving band that passes around the wheel and around a pulley, or whorl, on one end of the spindle. There are usually two grooves in the pulley, one deeper than the other. The band may ride in either groove, according to the amount of twist wanted in the yarn being spun. The deeper groove spins the yarn tighter. Some wool wheels have more than two grooves in the pulley.

The great wheel itself may or may not have a groove in which the single driving band rides. The driving band, which connects the great wheel to the spindle, is a length of cord that is spliced and waxed at the joining, or lapped and sewn. The joining is rubbed with beeswax or candle tallow. Use a cord for the driving band that stretches little,

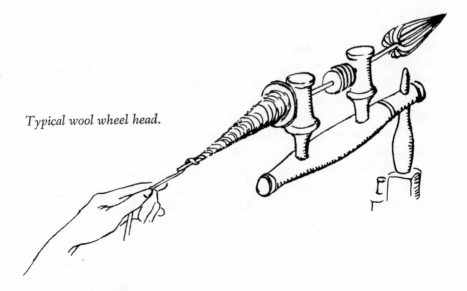

Typical wool wheel head.

such as staging cord or a woven cord, so that you are not always re-splicing the cord to shorten it.

The wheel is turned with the right hand or with a wooden wheel finger, or "wheel dolly," a stick about nine inches long that has a knob on one end to catch a spoke. Spokes of old wool wheels show wear at the top where they have been turned. Some old wool wheels have holes in the wheel spokes where pegs were inserted to make the large wheel into a reel for skeining the spun wool.

Various types of spinning heads are found on wool wheels. All are relatively simple devices for holding the spindle in a horizontal position in front of the wheel. The spindle may be suspended between two upright posts, resting in leather bearings or rawhide loops. Lacking rawhide, old mountain spinners used to make do with braided corn husks or string loops to secure the spindle. The spindle supported by two uprights dates earlier than the other types and is the typical wool wheel spinning head on antique wool wheels in the Midwest.

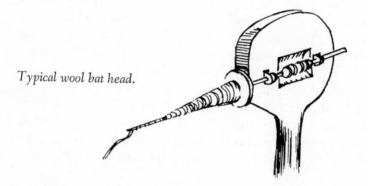

Typical wool bat head.

When the loops that hold the spindle horizontally are drawn through a wooden paddle back of the spindle, the spinning head is called a bat head. The bat head is seen in Canada and in the eastern United States, less frequently in the Midwest.

Some wool wheels have a small extra wheel mounted on the spinning head above the spindle. This is called "Miner's wheel," after the man who patented his invention at the beginning of the nineteenth century, or "speed wheel," after its function. The long driving band connecting the large wheel and the spinning head does not revolve the spindle directly, as usual. Instead, the driving band turns the Miner's wheel, which turns the spindle. Miner's wheel is connected to a small spindle pulley by its own short driving band.

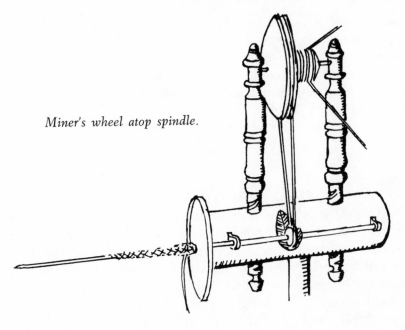

Miner's wheel atop spindle.

Curiously, old wool wheels in the Midwest do not have the small wheel mounted above the spindle. Miner's wheel seems to have remained a New England refinement of the wool wheel that failed to reach the pioneer outposts by the time home spinning began its decline. My spinning friend Mary Kennedy, who lives in Brandon, Vermont, writes:

> It is called, I believe, a "speed wheel." Early wool wheels do not have these small wheels. They appear to have been introduced about 1830 when a severe depression hit the East and many women returned to spinning their own wool. A friend has one labeled *Benjamin Pierre, Wheelheads, Chesterfield Factory, N. H.;* another has *Azel Wilder, Manufacturer,* on it. Having the small wheel connected to the pulley on the spindle makes spinning faster and smoother and one is able to do very fine, even spinning. Of the many wheels I have handled (twenty or so), all except one have been equipped with the speed wheel. They were very common here.

Adjusting Tension

The tension of the driving band that connects the great wheel to the spindle is adjusted below the spindle, either at the place where the spinning head is fastened to the bench or midway up the post that supports the mother-of-all. Loosening or tightening the tension screw merely moves the spinning head closer to the wheel or farther away, to loosen or tighten up the driving band as needed. The tension in the band should be just short of taut and such that the wheels turn easily and the band does not slip.

LUBRICATING THE WOOL WHEEL

If an old wool wheel is to run smoothly, the axle must be cleaned and lubricated. There is a small cotter pin or a wooden peg on the axle which can be removed so that the big wheel can be taken off. Inside, where the wheel revolves on the axle, there may be some dirty old grease if the spinning wheel has not been used recently. It should be removed. Scrape off the old grease, clean the metal axle with a solvent or an abrasive, or both, and replace the lubricant.

Perhaps the best lubricant to use on the axle is axle grease, a substance well known to farmers and mechanics but not one usually found in our homes.

Marion's husband, an architect, urged me to try it on my spinning wheel after he had used it to restore Marion's old wool wheel to smooth operation.

"After all," he said, laying a generous amount of grease on the axle, "axle grease is for axles, and that's an axle."

If you know a farmer or mechanic, it will be easy for you to obtain a small amount of axle grease, but you probably won't want to buy a whole can of it just to lubricate your wool wheel. You can also use Vaseline, lard, or candle grease mixed with powdered graphite. Make your own graphite by scraping the point of a lead pencil with a sharp knife. Vaseline, lard, and candle grease work very well, and we have them in our homes.

I like to light a candle and let a little candle grease drip on the graphite used to lubricate the axle of my wool wheel. After all, candle grease was the handiest thing to use in the old days. Candles were used to light the room where the great wool wheel stood at hearthside. It seems quite fitting to go on using candle tallow to keep my old wheel running smoothly. When it was new, in about 1760, candle tallow, or perhaps bear suet, was surely used to grease its axle.

How to Spin

Spinning is the process of simultaneously drawing out and twisting the rolag of fleece into a long, continuous filament. Before giving the fleece to the spindle, the beginner may wish to attenuate the rolag somewhat by drawing it out with the fingers into as long and thin a filament as possible without breaking the rolag. Spinning the yarn over the tip of the spindle will finish drawing out and twisting the rolag of fleece into a long, continuous filament. Attenuating the wool by hand before offering it to the spindle simplifies the spinning process and leaves less for the novice to do when the wheel is in operation. Later on, when the wheel works smoothly and the quality of yarn is satisfactory, the preliminary step of attenuating the yarn by hand should be abandoned and the fibers completely drawn out over the tip of the spindle.

Stand before the spinning wheel so that you can turn the wheel with your right hand while giving wool to the spindle with your left hand. Use the spokes to turn the large wheel with the right hand.

To begin, tie a length of spun yarn, about 12 inches long, onto the back of the empty spindle. This will provide a firm strand to which the newly spun yarn can be attached. Wind the spun yarn toward the point of the spindle so that there is only a short end of yarn hanging over the point. See below.

Spinning and winding positions of yarn.

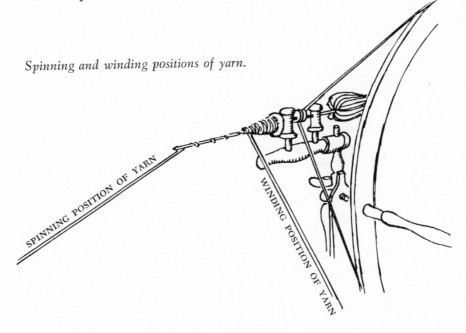

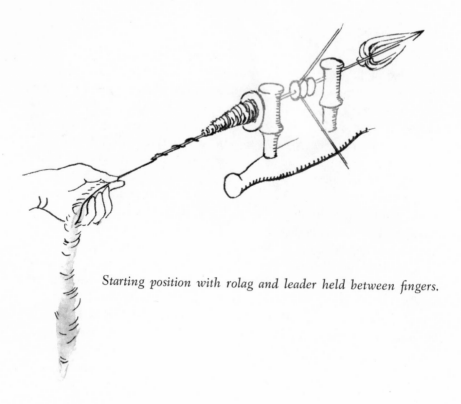

Starting position with rolag and leader held between fingers.

Fleece is spun off the tip of the spindle where the twisting occurs. Spun yarn is wound onto the back of the spindle near the pulley until the space is filled with a cone of spun wool.

Take a rolag of carded wool and spread out the fibers at one end of the sliver. Press the fibers at the end of the rolag around the end of the length of yarn hanging over the point of the spindle. Hold the unspun wool and the end of the spun yarn together with the thumb and fingers of the left hand. See above.

Slowly begin to turn the wheel clockwise with the right hand. At the same time, as the twist travels from the spun yarn on the tip of the spindle into the unspun fleece, release the wool through your fingers and pull out the fibers. Draw your left hand with the rolag of wool away from the spindle and almost straight out from the tip of the spindle. See facing page.

Allow as much wool to slip between your thumb and fingers as you find necessary to make yarn the thickness you desire. Do not allow

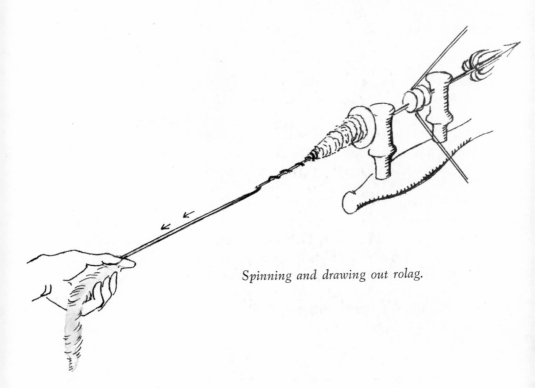

Spinning and drawing out rolag.

the twist to run past your thumb and fingers into the rolag of fleece held in your hand. Keep pulling out the fibers and holding back slightly until the twist runs down the yarn and you judge it to be spun satisfactorily. Do not hold back so much that the yarn becomes overtwisted and kinky.

The more the yarn is pulled out, the finer gauge it will be. Heavier yarn is less attenuated. At first your yarn will be thick and thin, with slubs and noticeable unevenness. Later on you will find that it is possible to spin yarn without slubs, all of one thickness. You may not, however, always want to spin such perfect yarn. The very charm of homespun lies in the slubs and in the variations of its size, which give interesting texture and a stout, hearty appearance to the yarn.

When you have drawn out the fibers in the manner described and have spun them over the tip of the spindle to a length of 18 to 24 inches, reverse the wheel enough to unwind the yarn at the end of the spindle. Then turn the wheel clockwise once more and wind up the spun yarn on the back of the spindle, holding the yarn at a right angle to the spindle shaft. See page 83.

Again wind the last end of the spun yarn down the length of the spindle so that it hangs over the point in the starting position and is ready for the remaining wool in the rolag to be drawn out over the tip of the spindle, as before.

When all the wool in the rolag is used, take another rolag and attach it to the end of the sliver in your hand and continue. If the yarn breaks during the spinning, lay the ends together in your hand and turn the wheel until the fibers are twisted together again.

As you draw out the fibers, keep your arm close to your body and step backward instead of standing in one spot and stretching your arm. At first you will be able to step backward only a step or two. As you become more skillful you will be able to turn the wheel and step backward three steps as you draw out the sliver. After a time you will develop a rhythm of movement that is graceful and regular—three steps backward while drawing out the fibers and three steps forward when winding the spun yarn onto the spindle.

The wheel is turned slowly while drawing out the fleece and reversing to unwind the yarn at the spindle tip, but may be turned quickly while winding the spun yarn onto the back of the spindle.

As the spindle fills with spun yarn, wind it onto the back of the spindle next to the pulley in the shape of a cone, leaving the tip of the spindle uncovered.

When the spindle is full, slip off the driving band and slowly wind the yarn off onto a reel, or niddy noddy, to make the skein (see Chapter 10). Do not empty the spindle completely from now on, because the yarn spins more easily at first if there is some yarn on the spindle.

Old-time spinsters used to wind a corn shuck on the back of the spindle shaft to form the center for each "broach," or spindleful, of yarn. Then, when the spindle was full, the broach of yarn was slipped off and laid by until the day's stint was done. The spinster saved the time of stopping to wind off each spindleful of yarn after it was spun and the skeining could be done all at once, perhaps when she sat resting on her vine-covered porch of evenings.

Step by Step

1. Tie a 12-inch piece of spun yarn to the empty spindle near the pulley.
2. Wind the spun yarn onto the spindle in a spiral that ends near the point of the spindle with a short end hanging over.
3. Attenuate a rolag of fleece with the fingers into as long and thin a filament as possible without breaking the rolag. (For beginning spinners only.)
4. Attach the rolag to the end of the spun yarn hanging over the spindle tip by pressing and twisting the ends together.
5. Hold wool together with thumb and fingers of the left hand while slowly turning the wheel clockwise with the right hand.
6. When the twist travels into the unspun fleece, release the wool through the fingers while pulling out the rolag. Keep the wool twisting over the tip of the spindle, drawing the left hand with the rolag away from the spindle's tip and almost straight out to the side until the length of yarn spun is 18 to 24 inches long.
7. Reverse the wheel part of a turn to unwind the spiral of yarn over the tip of the spindle.
8. Hold the spun yarn in the left hand in front of the spindle, turn the wheel clockwise, and wind the spun yarn onto the spindle next to the pulley in the shape of a cone.
9. Wind the last end of spun yarn onto the spindle in a spiral that ends on the tip of the spindle at the point where the rolag begins, or so that enough yarn is left with which to attach a new rolag if the old one is used up.

CHAPTER SEVEN

Spinning Wool
on a Treadle Wheel

The spinning wheel that spun the goldenrod yarn that enchanted my childhood—and enchants me still—was a flax wheel, circa 1840.

A flax wheel spins flax, but also wool fleece, cotton fibers, and silk. The spinster sits beside a low wheel and revolves it with a foot treadle that frees both hands to feed the fibers to the spindle. A flyer revolving around the spindle and bobbin winds the yarn onto the bobbin as fast as it is spun.

Grandmother's flax wheel was called a Saxony spinning wheel. Sometimes she said "my low wheel" or "the footwheel" to distinguish it from the high wheel or wool wheel. Hers was typical of the greatly improved spinning-wheel design with flyer, bobbin, and treadle that evolved from the wool wheel in the sixteenth century. The small driving wheel is mounted on the low end of a slanting three-legged bench above the treadle, and the improved spinning device is mounted at the upper end of the bench, where the distaff may also be mounted for flax spinning. See page 90.

The flyer and detachable bobbin added to spinning wheels, which brought the craft of handspinning to its zenith, are credited to a wood-carver, Johann Jurgen, from Brunswick, Germany. Drawings of Leonardo da Vinci, made before his death in 1519, show that he, too, had conceived a spinning-wheel flyer similar to the one Jurgen introduced later, about 1530, but da Vinci's invention was not brought into practical use.

Jurgen's flyer and the foot treadle made handspinning easier and faster. It became possible to spin yarn and wind it onto the spindle at the same time. The spinster no longer had to pause to wind up each arm's length of spun thread before drawing out another short length. Drawing out the fibers, twisting, and winding went on simultaneously and speedily without interruption. All the fibers—wool, flax, cotton, silk—could be spun on the same spinning device. New refinements of spinning were possible. One pound of wool could be spun out to unbelievable lengths while the spinster sat before the wheel in comfort. One spinster could spin as much flax on the efficient new wheel as six spinsters using the distaff and spindle. Fine cloth was available to everyone, not just those who possessed the greatest skill with hand spindle or wool wheel. Spinning became an important home industry.

The first spinning wheels equipped with Jurgen's flyer and bobbin, and a treadle, were called Brunswick wheels. As the new spinning-wheel design was adapted in other regions, sometimes with slight variations in slant of bench, angle and support of driving wheel, number of wheel spokes, or depth of wheel rim, it took other names—Saxony, low Irish, Dutch, Norwegian, and others.

Marion's hundred-and-fifty-year-old Bavarian parlor wheel is another type of treadle wheel, which has the same parts as those of the Saxony wheel, but is more compactly arranged in a vertical style. This type of upright spinning wheel, with the flyer above a small driving wheel mounted on a squared or rounded bench (or table) above the treadle, takes even less space in the home than the Saxony wheel. It is usually called a German, or parlor, wheel, but like all spinning wheels, it has other names. Its small size made it popular in small homes; thus it was the "cottage" wheel. Graceful design made it a handsome piece in the best room of the house, so it was the "parlor" wheel. It was easy to carry to a friend's home for an afternoon's spinning, so it was a "visiting" wheel. Sometimes there were two spindles above the wheel so that two persons could spin at one time, making it the friendship, lover's, or gossip, wheel.

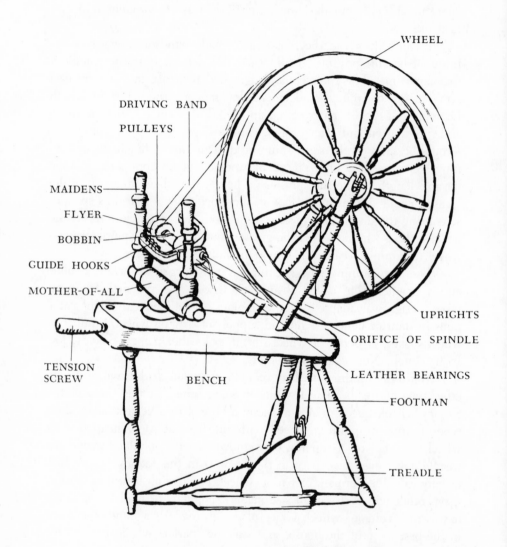

WHEEL

DRIVING BAND

PULLEYS

MAIDENS

FLYER

BOBBIN

GUIDE HOOKS

MOTHER-OF-ALL

TENSION
SCREW

BENCH

UPRIGHTS

ORIFICE OF SPINDLE

LEATHER BEARINGS

FOOTMAN

TREADLE

Saxony-type spinning wheel.

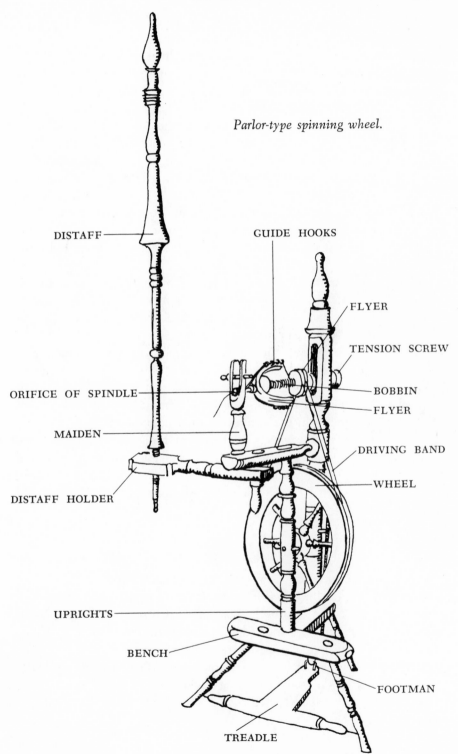

Parlor-type spinning wheel.

DISTAFF

GUIDE HOOKS

FLYER

TENSION SCREW

ORIFICE OF SPINDLE

BOBBIN

FLYER

MAIDEN

DRIVING BAND

DISTAFF HOLDER

WHEEL

UPRIGHTS

BENCH

FOOTMAN

TREADLE

The small parlor wheels were often very fancy. Marion believes that they were used for spinning at special times—when there was company in the house or when idle hands sought pastime—rather than for heavy, everyday spinning. It is easy to imagine a softly slippered foot on the tiny curved treadle of Marion's Bavarian parlor wheel and graceful, ladylike hands leisurely drawing down flax from a plumed, beribboned distaff. Tiny ivory finials decorate the top of the well-turned maidens and twinkle between the elaborate spokes of the delicate rosewood wheel. It is truly a fine wheel for a fine lady that has ivory finials carved from tusks of a prehistoric mastodon dug from the icy depths of a Siberian snowbank.

Today's spinner looking for an antique footwheel will find most often the Saxony-type wheels, fewer parlor wheels, and only rarely the unusual wheels such as the gossip wheel, Irish castle wheel, and chair wheel.

The castle spinning wheel was devised by ingenious Irish cottagers to take less floor space than the sprawling wool wheels and Saxony wheels. The compact, vertical spinning wheel revolves atop a tripod of tall legs with its flyer beneath it.

The chair wheel, another distinctive type of spinning wheel using Jurgen's flyer, but for wool spinning only, is supported within the framework of four straight legs that look like chair legs. My old chair wheel is Pennsylvania Dutch. Others came from different backgrounds but are rarely found in the antiquer's usual haunts.

All of the treadle wheels are excellent for wool spinning. If you fail to find an antique one, new ones are available. Saxony, parlor, and chair wheels are being manufactured again. Some are American made, others are imported. See "Helpful Information" for addresses of suppliers.

ADJUSTMENT AND CARE OF THE WHEEL

The wheel that turns the spinning mechanism is connected to the spindle by one continuous driving band that passes around the rim of the wheel twice, crossing itself. Sometimes two separate driving bands are used. The driving band rides in two pulleys at the back of the spindle and in two grooves on the rim of the wheel.

The pulleys are of different diameters, causing them to revolve at different speeds, the bobbin turning faster than the spindle and flyer. The pulley with the deeper groove (and smaller diameter) is nearer the bobbin and causes it to revolve; it is the bobbin pulley. The spindle pulley is the pulley with the shallow groove (and larger diameter) on the end of the spindle back of the bobbin; it revolves the spindle shaft and flyer.

Sometimes the spindle pulley has two grooves, one deeper than the other, to permit a finer adjustment. Use of the spindle pulley with the shallow groove (and larger diameter) makes a lightly twisted yarn, and this groove is often called the weft or woof groove. Use of the spindle pulley with the deeper groove (and smaller diameter) produces a firmer twist in the yarn, and this groove is often called the warp groove. The smaller diameter pulley (warp groove) is usually nearest the bobbin, but not always. Use the weft groove when spinning yarn by the worsted method, the warp groove for spinning yarn by the woolen method. Each revolution of the spindle and flyer makes one twist in the yarn being spun; thus the smaller-diameter spindle pulley makes more revolutions than the larger-diameter spindle pulley and hence more twists in a length of yarn.

The unequal rates of revolution of the bobbin and spindle pulleys make it possible for the thread to be twisted, drawn in, and wound on the bobbin at the same time.

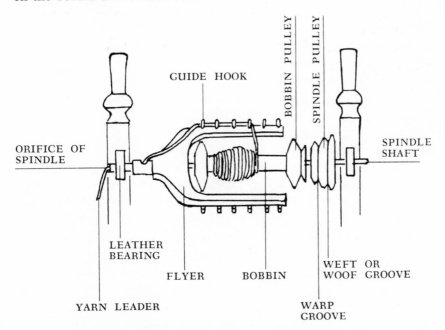

Spindle pulley with two grooves.

On treadle spinning wheels the tension on the driving band that turns the pulleys must be adjusted to a nicety by means of the tension screw. The tension screw moves the mother-of-all closer or farther away from the main wheel, which either tightens or slackens the tension of the driving band. To begin with, the tension of the driving band should be just short of taut, and the driving band should be spliced together so that this can be achieved with the tension screw in the middle turn. Both the amount of twist in the yarn spun and the speed at which the yarn is drawn through the orifice and wound onto the bobbin are affected by the tension of the driving band. The slightest variation in the tension adjustment causes subtle differences in the yarn and its spinning.

The driving band is a length of strong staging cord or a woven-type cord with little stretch, passed twice around the rim of the main wheel and through the pulleys, crossing itself. It is spliced or sewn together at the joining. The joining is rubbed with beeswax or tallow to make it smooth and to keep the spliced ends from unraveling.

Although one continuous driving band, crossing itself, is usual on treadle spinning wheels, two separate driving bands, each spliced and waxed at the joinings, may be used instead. I am using this arrangement at the present on my old Saxony wheel, which has only one groove on the spindle pulley. This can be a good arrangement if one of the pulleys is worn or when there is only one groove on the spindle pulley, which allows only one adjustment anyway.

The tension screw should be set on the middle turn when the driving bands are in place. It takes a bit of experimenting to determine exactly how long the driving band should be. After you have estimated this by passing the cord around the wheel twice, you must allow an extra two inches of cord for splicing or lapping and stitching. Chances are you will have to join the ends together several times before you have the band precisely the right length. It should be just short of taut, with the tension screw in the middle turn and the spliced ends joined smoothly.

Further adjustments of tension should be made while you spin. If the spinning yarn kinks up and refuses to pass through the orifice, tighten the tension a bit. When you begin to spin onto an empty bobbin, loosen the tension a bit, keeping in mind how much the tension screw was loosened. As the bobbin fills and the weight of the yarn slows down its speed of revolution, tighten up the bobbin screw just slightly, an eighth or a quarter of a turn after each round back and forth on the guide hooks, as required. Keep strict account of how much adjustment is made in order to keep the same ratio of wind-on to twist throughout a bobbinful of yarn.

While the thumps, groans, and squeaks of the spinning wheel are part of its own special music, too much noise from the wheel surely means that it is not working easily. It must be kept well lubricated if it is to run smoothly and reasonably quietly.

Before the driving bands are put into place, remove the wheel from its supports by taking out the peg that holds the axle shaft in place. An old wheel will be full of gummy old grease and dirt. There may also be some rust or rough spots on the metal axle shaft. Use a solvent such as turpentine or oleum to remove the grease. Rub the rough spots and rust with very fine sandpaper, a Brillo pad, or fine steel wool. Relubricate the axle with a generous amount of graphite mixed with Vaseline, lard, or candle grease. Replace the wheel. Put a dollop of the lubricant on the axle crank where it turns at the top of the footman.

If your wheel is old, the spindle should be cleaned too. To remove the spinning mechanism, twist the front maiden if it is not stationary, and the bobbin and flyer will be released. Remove the pulleys and slip the spindle shaft out of the leather bearing. If the maidens are stationary, simply bend the leather bearing that holds the front of the spindle so that it can be slipped out. Clean the grease and rust off the spindle shaft with solvent and abrasive, as described above, then polish the spindle shaft with metal polish such as Brasso. The guide hooks on the flyer may also need attention. Smooth off the rough places with fine sandpaper. Replace all the cleaned parts. Use a little sewing-machine oil to lubricate the leather bearings on the maidens that support both ends of the spindle.

Other points that should be lubricated to quiet squeaks and groans are the holes in the legs where the treadle bar is attached.

Every old spinning wheel has some squeaks and groans that are due to age and wear and cannot be reached with an oil can. Old spinning wheels tend to dry out, too, when kept in heated rooms in wintertime. One winter I placed my Saxony wheel directly in front of a heating outlet. Before I realized what was happening, the legs had become very loose in their sockets and complained loudly whenever I treadled the spinning wheel. I moved the wheel out of the steady draft of warm air at once, and when summer came with its frequently humid days, thanks to the nearby Ohio River, the loud squeaks faded away.

Because old spinning wheels tend to dry out and shrink in dry, heated air, it makes sense to feed the wood occasionally to replace what is lost. Make a solution of one-half turpentine and one-half boiled linseed oil. Wet a cloth with this mixture and wipe over the entire spinning wheel except the rim of the wheel and the grooves in the pulleys. These must not be oiled, finished, or varnished, because the driving band will slip on them if they are treated in any way. Leave the turpentine and linseed-oil mixture on the spinning wheel for at least twenty-four hours to allow it to soak into the wood. Then rub off the excess with a soft cloth. This procedure will keep the wood of an old spinning wheel looking mellow and will clean the finish. Repeat the process every month or two to keep the wood in good condition.

If you have a new finish put on your old spinning wheel by a professional furniture refinisher, or if you do it yourself, do not refinish the rim of the wheel or the grooves of the pulleys. You may, however, remove the old stain or finish from these parts, just as you remove them from the rest of the spinning wheel.

How to Spin Wool Yarn on a Treadle Wheel

To begin, tie a length of spun yarn about 18 to 24 inches long onto the back of the bobbin. Bring the yarn up over the first guide hook at the end of the flyer and pass it down the flyer through the rest of the hooks and out through the orifice, or eye, of the spindle. The guide hooks (also "hecks") on either side of the flyer may be used, but if the spindle has an eye on two sides, be sure to use the exit on the same side as the hooks you are using.

Use a small crochet hook or a bent wire to reach through the orifice of the spindle from the front to draw out the end of the yarn. And keep the crochet hook handy. You will need it every time you have to draw the yarn through the orifice, which, for beginners, is often— every time the yarn breaks or when the end of it spins out of your hands up through the orifice and onto the bobbin.

Take a rolag of carded fleece and draw a few fibers out from one end. Spread out the fibers in a fan shape on your left palm and lay the end of the spun yarn on them. Join the unspun fibers and the leader with a slight twist to the left and hold the joining between your left

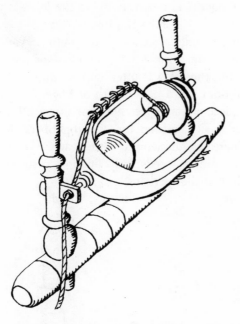

Spinning mechanism, showing threading of bobbin through guide hooks; ready to spin.

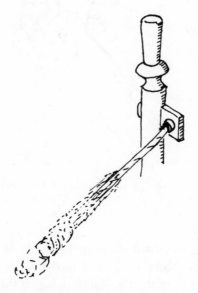

Rolag joined to leader a few inches below orifice.

thumb and forefinger. (The yarn twists to the left—"Z-twist"—when the wheel is turned clockwise for spinning.)

A beginning spinner needs a good length of yarn hanging out of the orifice because she cannot react rapidly enough when the wheel begins to turn and the rolag is often carried into the orifice before she has had time to draw out a new length of fibers for spinning. Allowing a long starting piece of yarn gives her time to get her right hand off the wheel and back to its position for drawing fibers from the rolag. As spinning skill increases, the length of the leader yarn may be shortened. An experienced spinner needs only enough yarn to attach the new rolag—two or three inches perhaps.

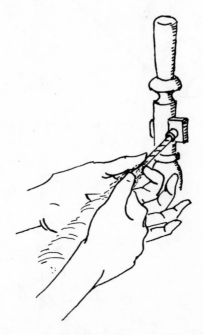

Starting position for spinning; left hand holding joining, right hand in position to draw.

Hold the rolag of carded fleece in the palm of the left hand with the place where the fibers are joined to the leader held between the thumb and forefinger. With the right hand give the wheel a clockwise turn and at the same time begin treadling slowly.

Here the beginner must learn to move quickly. "Hands fast, feet slow to spin" is the old rule. The length of spun yarn will move at once into the orifice and begin winding onto the bobbin. The left hand holding the rolag must move along toward the orifice with the starting (spun) yarn. If it holds back the yarn after it is spun, too much twist will accumulate and it will bunch up in a kinky mess that will not go through the eye of the spindle. As the left hand allows the spun yarn to go into the orifice, moving along with it slightly, the right hand, which started the wheel, must take hold of the rolag immediately behind the place where the left hand holds the rolag and begin drawing out the fibers from the rolag.

The spinning, or twisting, of the fibers into yarn takes place between the left hand and the spindle, and at the same time the drawing out of the fibers to regulate the size of the yarn spun takes place between the left hand and the right hand.

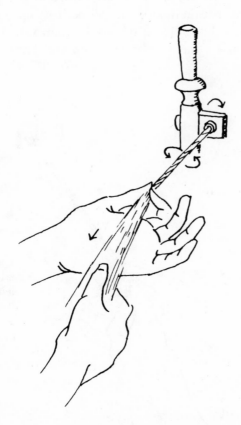

Left hand controlling twist, right hand drawing out fibers.

As soon as the starting yarn begins to wind onto the bobbin, move the left hand back several inches from the orifice of the flyer and release a short length of the drawn-out fibers between the thumb and fingers of the left hand. Then close the thumb and forefinger of the left hand and hold back slightly on this length of fibers for a moment, holding them just taut. This allows the twist, or spinning motion, to travel up the yarn from the point where it passes over the guide hook to the place where it is retained by the left hand. The trick is to hold the yarn just until the twist travels up to the thumb, then to release the twisted yarn and allow it to be carried into the orifice. As the twisted, or spun, yarn goes into the orifice and winds on the bobbin, the left hand again drops back several inches to control the next length of drawn-out fibers as the twist travels into them.

If you hold the fingers closed on the yarn too long, overtwist occurs, and your yarn will be too tightly twisted to be attractive. It may kink up so much that the spun yarn will not pass up through the spindle eye onto the bobbin. If you release the spun yarn *before* the twist travels up the fibers, the yarn is not spun and breaks or pulls apart easily.

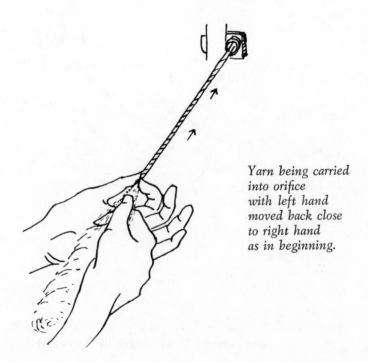

Yarn being carried into orifice with left hand moved back close to right hand as in beginning.

While the left hand controls the amount of twist in the yarn by alternately opening and closing the thumb and forefinger on the yarn, and feeds the spun yarn into the flyer to be wound onto the bobbin, the right hand must draw out the fibers from the rolag of fleece as quickly as each new length is needed.

While all this is going on, the foot must continue to pump the treadle at the right speed to keep the wheel going smoothly. The treadling must be absolutely steady and regular all the time, with an ankle-toe action rather than a tramping foot motion. Until the beginning spinner learns to treadle smoothly and automatically, it is almost impossible to concentrate on the work of the left hand and the work of the right hand. I suggest that the beginner first practice and master treadling the spinning wheel before ever attempting to handle the yarn. Try counting four beats to the bar or treadle to the tune of "Row, row, row your boat." The wheel has a maddening tendency to reverse direction for the novice. Always stop the wheel when the axle crank has just passed its highest point, so that it will not run backward.

After treadling has become automatic, attach a long piece of spun yarn to the flyer—even a whole ball of yarn—and practice winding the length of spun yarn onto the bobbin while treadling smoothly. Experiment with the spun yarn. Hold it back and watch the twist travel up the yarn to the thumb and finger of the left hand. Determine how long it can be held taut before it becomes too kinky to be taken into the orifice. When you practice with the spun yarn, put the driving band in the shallow groove of the spindle pulley—which is the pulley farthest from the bobbin with the larger diameter—so that there will be less twist added to the already spun yarn than if the driving band rests in the deeper groove of the spindle pulley.

When you master treadling and can judge when there is enough, too much, or too little twist in the yarn, you are ready to take on both the treadling and the handling of the rolag of carded fleece. Or perhaps you will want a companion to treadle while you practice with the fleece only.

You will soon discover that there is a definite rhythm to spinning on the treadle wheel—the holding back until the twist travels up the yarn to your fingers while you draw out the fibers with the other hand, the release of the fibers, the drag on the yarn as the motion of the flyer pulls the yarn into itself to be wound onto the spinning bobbin. Many women find this lyrical spinning rhythm, which comes from a synchrony of hand and foot and eye and mind to the steady beat of the treadle and the cadence of the whirring bobbin, a very tranquil and relaxing kind of domestic music.

When you finally catch on and feel the rhythm of spinning on the treadle wheel—and you will, perhaps quite easily—you will be able to perform all the basic motions of spinning without giving thought to each of them. Then you will be free to concentrate on the refinements of spinning that are possible with the treadle wheel or, perhaps, to let your mind soar on the cheering song of the spinning wheel.

STEP BY STEP

1. Tie a yarn leader, 18 to 24 inches long, onto the back of the bobbin. Bring the yarn up over the first hook on the flyer's tip, pass the yarn down the flyer through all the other hooks, and pull it out through the orifice of the spindle with a crochet hook.
2. Take a rolag of fleece and spread out a few fibers on one end. Lay the end of the leader on the fanned-out fibers of the rolag and twist them slightly to the left. Hold the joining between the closed thumb and forefinger of the left hand.
3. With the right hand give the wheel a clockwise turn and begin treadling slowly.
4. As the length of spun yarn begins to move at once into the orifice, winding up onto the bobbin, take hold of the rolag with the right hand immediately behind the left hand and begin drawing out the fibers of the rolag by moving the right hand back away from the left hand.
5. As the left hand moves nearer the orifice with the spun yarn being drawn onto the bobbin, open the thumb and forefinger of the left hand slightly and move it back on the drawn-out fibers until it is again close to the right hand. Again close the thumb and forefinger of the left hand and hold back slightly on the new length of fibers until the twist runs up the yarn to the thumb.
6. Meanwhile, with the right hand draw out a new length of fibers from the rolag.
7. As soon as the twist reaches the thumb of the left hand, stop holding back and let the left hand be carried toward the orifice as the yarn goes in.

8. Open the fingers of the left hand and let it drop back again several inches to the place where the right hand holds the rolag and allow the twist to run up into the new length of drawn-out fibers.

9. Repeat, adding a new rolag when the old one is used. Each time a rolag is joined on, move the yarn to the next guide hook on the flyer. After each complete round of the bobbin, down all the hooks and back up, tighten the tension screw very slightly, perhaps even less than a quarter of a turn for each round. Otherwise the increasing weight of the filling bobbin slows it down and changes the ratio of wind-on to twist. If you fail to adjust the tension to compensate for the change in speed of the bobbin revolutions, the yarn spun earlier on the empty bobbin will differ somewhat from that spun on the heavier bobbin.

WOOLEN AND WORSTED METHODS
OF SPINNING

The above method of spinning on a treadle spinning wheel is the woolen method of spinning yarn. Woolen yarn is spun from a rolag made of carded wool. The fibers used for woolen yarn are usually about 4 inches long, or shorter, although longer fibers may be prepared and spun by this method. Carding the fibers straightens them and makes them all lie in one direction, but when the rolag is rolled, the fibers in the airy roll are rearranged, so that they end up at cross angles to each other. Woolen yarns are fuzzy and soft because the fibers do not lie compactly parallel within the twisted strand. Since the fibers are short, the twist used to spin woolen yarn should be firm enough to provide strength, but not so tight that the soft, lofty, quality is lost. Spin woolen yarn with a slightly loosened tension and use a short draw to avoid pulling the short-fibered rolag apart. If there are two grooves in the spindle pulley, slip the driving band into the deeper groove (smaller-diameter pulley, or warp pulley) to twist the yarn firmly.

Only long fibers are spun by the worsted method. The very long fibers are usually combed. (See Chapter 5.) Those fibers that are not too long to be handled on the carders may be carded, but the rolag is rolled across the carder, from side to side, so that all the long fibers remain parallel to each other. Clean, well-teased longwools may be spun directly from the lock of fleece without combing or carding. Short fibers, called noils, are removed from the fleece during combing and are not spun into worsted yarns. The worsted method of spinning also differs from the woolen method in the way the long fibers are drawn out of the fleece. In woolen spinning the left hand is used in the forward position near the orifice of the spindle with the right hand moving back away from it while drawing out the fibers from the rolag. The left hand also moves back from the orifice when allowing the twist to run up into the newly drawn-out fibers. In worsted spinning the hands change positions; the left hand takes the back position, where it remains stationary about 6 inches from the orifice of the spindle, holding the lock of longwool fleece; the right hand works between the left hand and the orifice, drawing the fibers out from the lock of fleece, slightly sideways and toward the orifice, where they twist onto the spinning yarn being drawn onto the bobbin. For the longwool fibers spun by the worsted method, only enough twist to hold the fibers together is necessary. For a long, loose twist, put the driving band into the shallow groove of the spindle pulley (the larger-diameter, or weft, pulley) and tighten the tension to draw the yarn onto the bobbin at a fairly fast rate.

CHAPTER EIGHT

Spinning with a Hand Spindle

She layeth her hands to the spindle, and her hands hold the distaff.

—Proverbs XXXI:19

The beginnings of spinning, like those of other primeval discoveries, are lost in an abyss of antiquity. Early man used fire, rude implements, language, learned to farm, weave, and spin thousands of years before he became civilized enough to leave a record of his culture for posterity. How each elemental skill and occupation developed in the eons during which man's way of life changed from nomadic to agrarian is largely a matter of conjecture.

It is likely that Neolithic tribes practiced weaving before spinning was learned. Interlacing twigs and grasses to make useful items is a natural solution of a reasoning human trying to survive in a wilderness. The simple discovery by a clever Stone Age inhabitant that animal fibers twisted together became longer and stronger, making a stuff that could be woven, was the first step in development of the textile crafts and the domestication of wool-bearing animals.

By the time the Egyptians and Greeks had immortalized their lives and times in vivid pictorial and written histories, the utilitarian handcrafts of spinning yarns, weaving fabrics, and dyeing cloth had

Egyptian spinning on spindle.

advanced to a zenith of perfection that, in some ways, has not been reached since. The excellence of skill achieved in textile handcrafts of early cultures is apparent in displays of Egyptian artifacts in museums. Remnants of silky, gossamer linen cloth and mummy shrouds of finely woven ramie, perfectly preserved through the ages by the protective atmosphere of desert tombs of Egyptian kings, astound today's craftsmen. The quality of fiber, delicacy of yarn, expert weaving, and traces of still lovely dyes are remarkable when one realizes that only equipment we regard as primitive existed for use in Egyptian textile production five thousand years ago. From earliest times until the appearance of the spinning wheel around the thirteenth century the only tool used to aid in the spinning of fibers, even the fine Egyptian spinning, was the simple hand spindle.

In the very beginning, spinning was done without tools. The thread was drawn out of a bundle of fibers and twisted between the fingers or between the palm of one hand and the leg. The length of "spun" thread was then wound onto a short, straight stick, and another length was spun. From this spinning stick the hand spindle developed.

In time the spinning stick was notched to hold the thread, and a weight was added to the bottom to give it momentum as it rotated and twisted the thread. The weight, known as the whorl, was a piece of clay, a round piece of wood, or a flat rock. Now the drawing out of the fibers and the twisting were done at the same time, one hand rotating the spindle, one hand drawing the fibers.

With these improvements, the spindle became a handy implement to spinning. The good housewife, who kept her fingers ever busy at the spindle, could spin anytime, anywhere—even while outdoors—sitting or walking. Children, too, given the chores of baby-tending or herding sheep, passed the time making thread on the spindle for the family's household goods.

The supply of flax or fleece to be spun by the housewife while she was away from home was tied to a long, cleft staff, which was tucked under her sash, held under her arm, or slung from her shoulder, so that she could pull the fibers out continuously as she walked and spun. This staff, bound with unspun flax or fleece, is the distaff, companion to the hand spindle in antiquity. The word "distaff" comes from the Old English *distæf, dis* meaning a bunch of flax. In Old German *Dise* meant flax, from which comes the verb *dizen,* meaning to dress the distaff with flax. The term "distaff side" is still a proper legal term to designate the female line or maternal branch of a family.

Spinning with spindle and distaff was so exclusively the female duty that the word "distaff" came also to mean woman, or women in general.

From the German *Rocken,* which means "distaff" (as well as "woman's"), came the long-used phrase "spinning on the rock" and the name of the ancient English holiday, Rock Day, or St. Distaff's Day,

"Spinning on the rock."

Firing the tow on St. Distaff's Day.

which fell on January 7. Rock Day followed Twelfth Night, which marked the end of Christmas merrymaking. On this day the maids were expected to resume their constant chore of spinning. The plough-men, however, were free until Plough Day, the first Monday following Twelfth Night. In the meantime they amused themselves by playing pranks on the spinning maids. Herrick describes the traditional pranks of Rock Day:

> Partly work and partly play
> You must on St. Distaff's Day:
> From the plough soon free your team;
> Then come home and fother them:
> If the maids a-spinning go,
> Burn the flax and fire the tow.
> Bring in pails of water then,
> Let the maids bewash the men.
> Give St. Distaff all the right:
> Then bid Christmas sport good night,
> And next morrow every one
> To his own vocation.

Distaffs and spindles, though utterly simple in their basic design, exist in varied forms. Spindles may be tiny, a few inches long with a lightweight whorl, for spinning delicate threads, or more than two feet long with a thick disc, as the Navajo spindles. An average spindle is a slender, tapered piece of wood about a foot long, with a thin flat whorl near the bottom portion of the spindle and a notch at the top

of the spindle. Most spindles are plain and unornamented, but distaffs are often quite decorative. A distaff might be of gracefully tapered carved wood with a tiny quaint figure at the top. Others have a circle of shaped tines surrounding the center post; these distaffs may be called tow forks. The poor man's counterpart of the decorative tow fork is a branch of a tree that ends in a witch's broom of switches. The tips of the switches are bound together, making a form to fasten the flax or fleece onto.

Later the distaff was mounted on its own stool to keep the supply of fibers ready at the fireside for the mistress of the house as she sat spinning. Much later the distaff was mounted on the swinging arm of a post above the spinning wheel.

There are several methods of spindle spinning. When the spinster spins while standing or walking about, she holds the distaff under her left arm, leaving both hands free to draw the fibers and control the spindle. She draws out wisps of unspun fibers from the distaff and fastens them to the spun thread twisting up the spindle through the notch at the spindle top. With her right hand she gives the spindle a brisk clockwise twirl and lets it fall, gyrating, toward the ground. She holds the twisting thread between the fingers of her right hand, letting it slip through as the twist meets her fingers, and deftly pulls more fibers from the distaff with her left hand all the while, to give more length to the thread being spun by the gyrating spindle. When the dangling, twirling spindle reaches the ground the spinster pauses and quickly winds the spun thread around the palm of her right hand as she bends to pick up the fallen spindle. She then winds the new-spun thread onto the spindle near the whorl and secures the end of it in the notch, ready to begin again. The spindle used for this type of spinning is also known as a drop spindle or a free spindle.

How wearisome spinning must have been in bygone days, when a spinner's fingers could not be idle, even on a foot journey.

Indoors, while sitting at the hearthside, spinners often set the tip of the spindle twirling, like a top, in a groove hollowed out in the hearthstone. A small bowl, or even a coconut shell—the still-used method of primitive people—works equally well. The spinner draws the fibers up from the twirling spindle as the thread is spun, the reverse of the drop-spindle method. Twirling the spindle in a bowl works better when spinning thin yarns that will not bear the weight of the falling spindle.

The long Navajo spindle, called a *beedizi,* is slanted against the spinner's right thigh as she sits on a low rock or on the ground. The spindle is rolled against the thigh with the palm of the right hand while the yarn is spun over the point of the spindle tip, which is not notched. The left hand pulls out the fibers from the wool sliver. Sometimes the point of the *beedizi* is spun in a little cup on the ground. Sometimes the left leg is doubled under the right thigh and the spindle is held between the toes of the left foot.

Navajo woman spinning.

How to Spin Wool Yarn with a Drop (Hand) Spindle—Method I

1. Attach a length of spun yarn, about a yard long, to the spindle. Tie the yarn to the spindle shaft above the whorl. Wind it around the spindle near the whorl several times, then pass the yarn down over the edge of the whorl, underneath it, around the spindle shaft under the whorl, and back up the side of the spindle to the top.
2. Fasten the end of the spun yarn in the notch at the upper end of the spindle with a half hitch, leaving an end of the spun yarn free above the tip of the spindle to fasten to the wool fibers, about 3 inches, or perhaps more for the beginner.

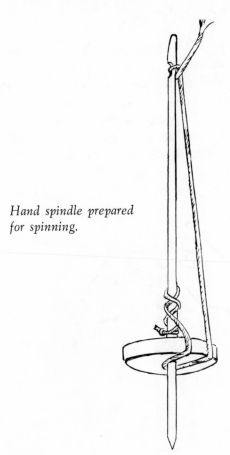

Hand spindle prepared for spinning.

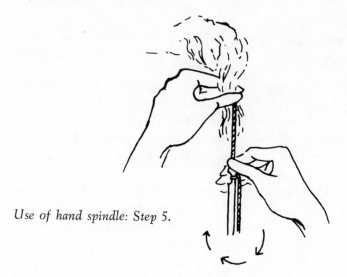

Use of hand spindle: Step 5.

3. Draw out and wrap a few fibers from the lock of fleece (or rolag) around the end of the spun yarn, using a Z-twist.
4. Hold the joining of the spun yarn and the fleece between the left finger and thumb, letting the spindle dangle from the yarn.
5. With the right hand give the spindle a clockwise spin.
6. Quickly move the right hand up and close the finger and thumb on the yarn and fleece immediately below the left hand.

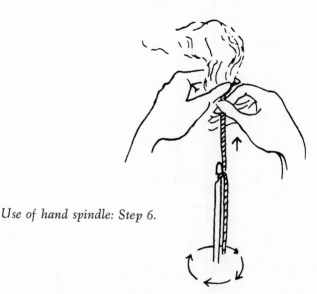

Use of hand spindle: Step 6.

7. As soon as the right hand closes on the yarn and fibers, preventing the twist forming below the hands from running up into the unspun wool, move the left hand upward about 2 inches away from the right hand, drawing out a few more fibers.

8. Then *close* the finger and thumb of the left hand on the fibers and *release* the thumb of the right hand, allowing the twist formed by the revolving spindle to run up into the short length of unspun fibers just drawn out.

9. Keep the spindle twirling in the clockwise direction while continuing to draw out the fibers and control the twist as described. The spindle must not be allowed to reverse direction or the twist you have just put into the yarn will unwind. To prevent this, rest the spindle where it will remain stationary as soon as it stops twirling. Beginners will find it easier to spin with the drop spindle while sitting on a chair rather than while standing; then the dangling spindle can be held between the knees when it stops twirling before it reaches the floor.

10. When the spindle touches the floor, pick it up with the left hand and wind the length of newly spun yarn around the fingers of the right hand.

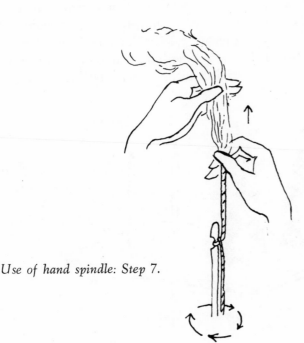

Use of hand spindle: Step 7.

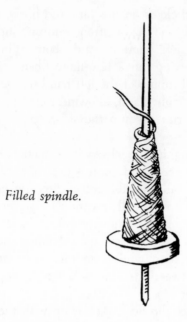

Filled spindle.

11. Slip the half hitch over the tip of the spindle and remove the yarn from under the whorl. Begin winding the spun yarn onto the spindle at the place where it is tied on near the whorl, winding it up the spindle shaft about 3 inches in a spiral, then winding it back down in a spiral, which crisscrosses the yarn. Wind it back up again and down, ending each round of wound yarn a bit higher up on

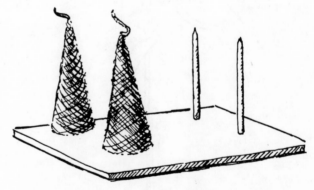

Cones of yarn on holder.

the spindle shaft than the last round. This fills the lower part of the spindle above the whorl with a tidy cone of spun yarn and keeps the spindle balanced, so that it twirls evenly.

12. Rethread the spindle (steps 1 and 2) and repeat the procedure.
13. When the spindle is filled, push up the whorl, if it is removable, and take off the cone of spun yarn.
14. Skein the yarn (see Chapter 10) or place the cone on a holder for plying. Make the holder of spikes (pencils, sucker sticks, knitting needles, long nails) pushed through a square of thin wood or heavy cardboard.

When You Become Adept at Spindle Spinning:

A. Reduce the length of spun yarn left free above the spindle tip (step 2) to only an inch or two.
B. Gradually increase the short length of unspun fibers drawn out from the fleece with the left hand (step 8) from 2 inches to a longer draw, 4 or 5 inches if the staple length of the wool fiber permits.
C. Allow some twist to run up into the unspun fleece *as it is drawn out* instead of keeping the thumb and finger of the right hand tightly closed on the fibers until the drawing out is finished (steps 8 & 9).

Note: In the procedure above, the left hand draws out the fibers and the right hand twirls the spindle and controls the twist in the spinning yarn. This is traditional in hand-spindle spinning, because the left hand was always used to draw down fibers from a distaff held under the left arm. However, the traditional functions of the right and left hands in "spinning on the rock" are opposite to the functions of the right and left hand when spinning wool on the Saxony wheel and naturally seem a bit awkward to right-handed people, who find it easier to use the most dexterous hand for the most difficult of the two tasks, that of drawing out the fiber. For that reason I suggest that the beginner switch hands, using the right hand for drawing out the fibers and the left hand for controlling the twist and twirling the spindle, if it seems less awkward.

DIRECTION OF TWIST IN SPUN YARN

Yarn spun with the drop spindle twirling in the clockwise direction is left, or Z-twisted, yarn. To make an S-twisted yarn, which twists to the right, the spindle must be twirled in a counterclockwise direction.

SPINNING WOOL YARN WITH A HAND SPINDLE —METHOD II

Yarn can be spun on the hand spindle without dropping it to the ground and with the spinner sitting instead of standing. The end of the spindle is placed in a small bowl, groove, coconut shell, or in its own spinning base, which is placed on the floor beside the spinner, on a low stool, or on the table in front of the spinner. The fiber to be

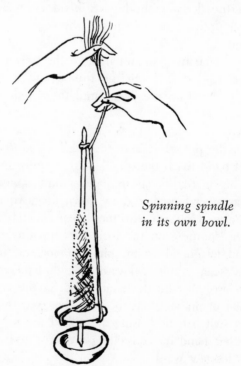

Spinning spindle in its own bowl.

spun is kept nearby in a basket or drawn from a distaff mounted on its own three-legged stool.

Drafting and spinning of the fibers is done as with the drop spindle except that the spinner draws the thread upward from the spindle—which remains on its base spinning like a top—raising her arms to draw out the length of yarn instead of dropping the spindle toward the ground. The weight of the spindle plays a smaller part in the spinning by this method, although the weight of the spinning spindle provides some tension. The lower hand, usually the right hand, twirls the spindle, and the left, or upper, hand, draws the fibers upward with the finger and thumb slightly open; the lower hand controls the twist in the usual way.

The yarn spun with the spindle spinning like a top does not bear the weight of the falling spindle, so finer fibers can be spun this way without breaking under the weight of the dangling spindle. Cotton is spun by this method. The "woven wind" cottons of India—delicate, spiderweb threads—were spun on miniature spindles, which twirled in a bowl of water to provide proper humidity. The spinning-top method is good, too, for woolen spinning of rolags made of short, fine fibers.

Spinning Wool Yarn with a Navaho *Beedizi*

The Navajo *beedizi* is a large spindle at least 20 inches long (mine is 26″ long), weighted with a large whorl 4 or 5 inches in diameter. It spins a heavy yarn, so the wool fiber used should be long and coarse. For rug warp or to give the yarn greater strength, spin it a second time. The Navahos have a breed of sheep, the Navajo, that produces extremely coarse wool used almost exclusively in the production of their blankets and rugs.

Sit on a chair, rather than on the ground as the Navaho spinner might, so that the top of the *beedizi* is leaned against the right leg above the knee. Put the tip of the spindle in a depression in a rock, piece of wood, or bowl, so that it will spin like a top retained in one place.

1. Attach a piece of strong wool yarn to the spindle just above the whorl. Wind it in a spiral up the spindle shaft to within 1 inch

Navajo beedizi.

from the tip. At this point wind the yarn closely around the tip three or four times and let 3 inches of spun yarn extend beyond the spindle tip. Untwist the fibers at the end of the spun yarn.

2. Attenuate and fan out the fibers at one end of the rolag of wool. Join these fibers to the frayed ends of spun yarn extending over the spindle tip.

3. Hold the joining of the spun yarn and the rolag with the thumb and forefinger of the left hand. With the palm of the right hand begin to roll the shaft of the spindle clockwise on the right thigh, using the hand in a backward-stroking motion.

4. As the spindle revolves, hold the yarn at the joining until the twist forms in the fibers at the end of the spindle. Then open the thumb and forefinger and move the left hand back a short distance on the yarn while drawing out the new length of fibers to make the size of yarn wanted and allowing the twist to move up.

5. Keep the thumb and forefinger closed on the yarn until enough twist forms, then move the left hand back again, pulling out more fibers from the rolag for spinning.

6. When an arm's length of yarn is spun, stop rolling the spindle with the right hand and wind the new-spun yarn on the spindle near the whorl as in Step 11 for the drop spindle.

7. Repeat the procedure, joining on new rolags as needed.

CHAPTER NINE

Spinning Flax and Other Fibers

Deceite, weepying, spynnyng God hath yive
To wommen kyndely, whil that they may lyve.

—Chaucer,
The Prologue to the Wife of Bath's Tale,
Canterbury Tales

Once the challenge of wool spinning has been met, spinners, to the last one, begin to look for variety in the spinning of threads from other fibers. The first choice after wool is often flax.

Flax is not as easily obtained as wool fleece. Today's spinner cannot buy it from the farmer down the lane, as wool might be bought, although there was a time when the opposite was true. In the early days of the country every farmer raised flax, but few owned sheep.

An old history of Warrick County, Indiana, describes the clothing worn by the pioneers here in the early days of the settlement of the county, which was begun in 1803 at Newburgh, where I live.

The prevailing dress for men in the very earliest days of the settlements consisted of a hunting shirt, made either of tow-linen or linsey, with under-clothing of the same material, and if their pants were not made of the same they would be buckskin. Their heads were mostly covered with a cap made of the skin of some wild animal, and their shoes, if they had any, were made from leather tanned in the vicinity, and almost every farmer was his own cord-wainer and cobbler. Very often the boys, until they were in their teens, would never be the possessor of a pair of shoes, and their feet would become like hoofs. Every farmer would have his flax-patch, which would generally consist of a quarter or half an acre. When it ripened it had to be pulled, cured, seeded, rotted, broke, swingled, hackled, spun, and woven, all by hand, and mostly by the women, before it was ready to be made into wearing apparel. One feat at spinning was often done by those early mothers that none of the modern young mothers can accomplish. They would, with one foot, rock the cradle at their side, with an infant in it, while with the other they turned the spinning-wheel; holding another child in their arms, while with their fingers they took the flax from the distaff and prepared it for thread. Cotton goods for shirts, dresses, or any kind of clothing, was a luxury rarely indulged in—it was all linen, even the buttons for their shirts were made of linen thread. If some young lady or gentleman, more ambitious than others, should indulge in a suit of "store clothes," they had to pay dearly for them; also stand the envy and jeers of their companions.

Homespun linens, plain and closely woven, were a testimony to months of arduous toil for both the farmer and his wife, beginning with the planting of the flax. Flax was the common, everyday textile fiber—wool, cotton, and silk the rare ones.

The tall flax plant with its pretty blue flowers that once was so familiar would go unrecognized today. The spinner who needs flax for her distaff must buy it from one of the commercial suppliers, who import it from countries where flax production is still an industry. It is supplied in bundles (stricks) of flax fibers that have been dressed for spinning, or in a long, continuous, ribbonlike strip called a top. If the top is cut into smaller pieces, the flax is called cut flax. The strick of flax is spun from a distaff; the flax top is spun from the hands without a distaff.

Proper dressing of the flax includes curing, rippling, retting, grassing, scutching, and hackling, which separate the seeds, outer fibers, and waste from the long (line) and short (tow) fibers of flax.

DRESSING THE DISTAFF FOR FLAX SPINNING

A small portion of the strick of flax is attached to a distaff for spinning. This must be done very carefully, in a certain manner, or the long fibers cannot be pulled out of the flax bundle for spinning without tangling the remaining fibers on the distaff.

First, hold the strick firmly by one end and shake it out. Remove about 2 ounces of flax from one side of the bundle, being careful not to disturb the remainder. If bits of boon remain in the flax, use a metal dog comb to comb out the rest of it.

Now tie a piece of string around your waist, knotting it in front of you, leaving two ends to tie around one end of the piece of flax you have just separated from the strick. When the flax is tied firmly to your waist, clip off the ends of string so that they do not tangle in the flax.

Sit on a chair, a cloth spread over your knees, and lay the piece of flax in the center of your lap. Take hold of the flax with your left hand opposite the end that is tied to your waist.

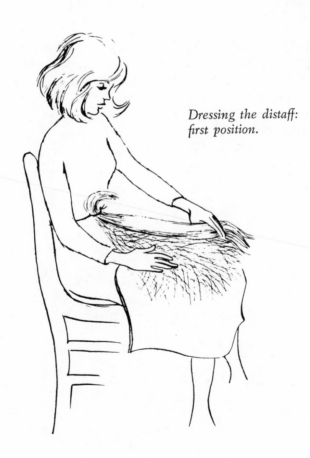

Dressing the distaff: first position.

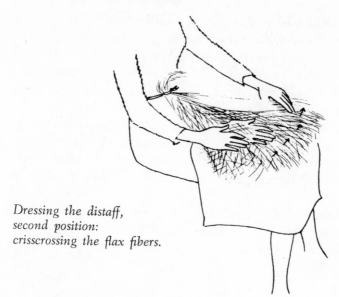

*Dressing the distaff,
second position:
crisscrossing the flax fibers.*

Beginning with the strick of flax held a few inches above the right knee, pull down a bit of flax and hold it on your knee with the flat of the right hand while you slowly move your left hand a bit more toward the left. The fibers of flax must be spread out like a web on your lap so that all are crisscrossed and none lie straight. As your left hand moves over toward the left knee, move the palm of the hand, holding the spreading fibers down on your lap, until the lap is filled with a thin, fan-shaped web of flax.

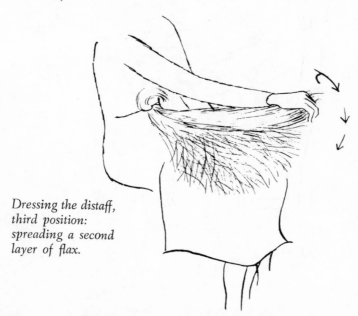

*Dressing the distaff,
third position:
spreading a second
layer of flax.*

Then reverse hands, using the right hand to hold the strick and the left one to spread the flax. Start back across the lap in the opposite direction, spreading another thin layer of flax on top of the first one. Do this again and again until all the flax is spread, in one continuous layer folded back upon itself at the edges of the fan time after time, with all the fibers crossing each other.

Cut the string at your waist that holds the top of the web of flax. Loosen the flax at the top where it was tied and fold up any loose ends at the bottom of the web where it hangs over the knees.

Lift the flax off your lap and place it on a flat surface. Place the distaff on the right-hand edge of the fan of flax, with the top of the distaff where the string tied it to your waist. With the right hand wind the flax slowly around the distaff, keeping the top of the distaff on the same place at the top of the fan, pivoting the distaff around to the left, winding it tighter at the top than at the bottom, which will have a larger circumference than the top. Pat the joining together and tuck up the bottom of the flax, which forms a cone at the top of the distaff. Place the distaff in its holder.

Take a length of narrow ribbon, about 2 yards long, and tie the center of it around the flax at the top of the distaff, then crisscross the

Winding the flax around the distaff.

ribbons down and around the cone of flax, ending with a bow at the bottom. Make a plume out of the ends at the top of the distaff finial, and the distaff is dressed, ready for spinning.

The bundle of flax fibers to be fanned out across the knees cannot be longer than arm's length, since one must be able to grasp the flax at the end opposite the end tied to the waist. If the bundle of flax is longer (and it might well be 36 inches long), and you wish to bedizen the distaff with the entire length—a long, handsome, fairy-tale mane of flax—you will need to adapt the fanning method described above. Instead, tie one end of the flax bundle to the bed post and fan out the flax fibers on the bed in front of you.

Almost all difficulties in flax spinning come from an improperly dressed distaff, so do not be careless in its preparation.

SPINNING FLAX FROM THE DISTAFF ON A SPINNING WHEEL

Have the distaff to the left and almost in front of the orifice of the spinning wheel. Keep a small cup of water or a wet sponge on the bench of the spinning wheel to dampen your left thumb and fore-finger. Many antique wheels have a place for the water container, which has long since disappeared. Old-time spinners hung a gourd on the spinning wheel to hold the water if there was no place to set the cup.

Starting with the lowest hanging bit of flax, pull down a few fibers and twist them onto the leader yarn brought up from the bobbin. Give the wheel a clockwise turn and begin treadling very slowly. Keep the left hand a few inches below the bottom of the distaff, the thumb and forefinger always lightly closed on the flax. Continue drawing down a few fibers at a time from the bottom of the cone of flax by a slight twisting of the dampened thumb and forefinger toward the wheel. Each time the thumb and finger twist the fibers, a few fresh strands from the distaff catch onto the twisting thread, and in this way the thickness of the thread is determined.

While the left hand controls the drawing, the right hand smooths away irregularities in the thread twisting below the left hand. It moves upward on the thread, away from the orifice and toward the distaff.

When the left hand again needs dampening, the right hand takes over guiding and twisting the fibers at the distaff.

The twist in the thread being spun is kept below the left thumb and finger. If it is allowed to run above the fingers, too many fibers from the distaff will be caught up at once.

The distaff must be turned around a little after each few minutes' spinning so that the fibers are drawn down evenly all around the cone of flax. As the flax is used up to the lower crisscross of the ribbon, retie the bow higher up.

The tension of the spinning wheel should be kept loose and the treadling done very slowly. Flax must be handled very lightly and unhurriedly. It needs only to be twisted enough to provide strength. As soon as the flax twists into a thread, allow it to pass onto the bobbin. Do not hold it back.

Flax thread spun with damp fingers will be smooth and glossy. Dry-spun yarn will be rough and uneven, with hairy whiskers. Coarse linen fibers should be spun into a thick thread. Fine linen may be spun either fine or thick, according to the use for which it is intended.

Spinning Flax Top

Flax top and cut flax are spun from the hand like wool. Thread can be spun directly out of the cut flax bundles unless they are a bit too thick and need dividing.

Flax top is prepared as follows: Pull off the uncut top a piece about 18 inches long. Divide this portion in halves the long way. Take one of the half portions and carefully draw it out by hand, pulling out a few inches at a time, starting at one end of the top and working down to the other end until it is at least double the length it was. The hands are kept close together while the top is being attenuated, with one hand pulling opposite the other. Allow the sliver of flax to coil into your lap. Do not pick it up after the entire length has been elongated but spin it at once, drafting and spinning from the coil in your lap.

The sliver of flax top is held as for wool spinning, with the right hand forward and the left hand controlling the draft. The moistened thumb and index finger of the right hand are kept lightly closed on the flax sliver, and, as the fibers twist between the fingers, draw up the twisting fibers toward you to smooth in whiskers sticking out of the yarn.

When the sliver runs out, draw out another length of flax top and join it to an untwisted portion of the old sliver, using a few Z-twists made with a wet finger.

SPINNING TOW

The short fibers of flax that are left when the flax is hackled are called tow. Tow may be combed separately and spun for weft thread for weaving.

Comb the tow flax with a fine-toothed flax hackle, if you have one, or a metal dog comb. Final combing may be given the tow with a hair comb. When it is smooth, twist the tow into a roving about the size of the little finger by drawing out the fibers and twisting them a bit toward the left.

Lace the roving around the prongs of a tow fork for spinning, or roll the roving into a ball, which may be held on the lap during spinning.

Tow fork with flax rovings.

Spin the tow as you would spin worsted yarn, with a loose twist. Draw out the fibers with the right hand and smooth them back toward the roving as they twist. Keep the thumb and forefinger damp, as when spinning flax line.

SPINNING OTHER FIBERS

DOG HAIR

I remember Brother Kim's pride in the rather scratchy but interesting-looking cap he had spun and knitted from the hair of a shaggy white dog, which he showed us on one of our evening excursions to the monastery when we four housewives were learning to spin. We laughed when Mary Jane wondered if the cap would smell like wet dog if Brother Kim was caught wearing it in the rain. Right then I resolved, privately, to stick to wool spinning, which was odoriferous enough for me.

But here I am, true to spinning prototype, combing the family dog with more thought of the combings than of the dog's grooming. The hair of certain dogs spins up very well, making nice yarn alone or combed into wool. And the dog smell disappears as soon as the yarn is washed.

Poodle clippings make a good woolly yarn that is interesting in color. Dog hair that is harder and more lustrous makes a worsted-type yarn. The hair of the Husky-type Samoyed dog is prized by spinners and may be bought occasionally from dealers who supply knitting and spinning wools. Newfoundland dog hair makes a beautiful, soft, angoralike yarn.

Dog hair needs oil added to it before carding and spinning. See Chapter 5. Some time may pass before enough combings and clippings accumulate for spinning, so store them in the meantime in a large glass jar with a tight lid.

NOVELTY ANIMAL FIBERS FOR SPINNING

Other animal fibers, such as camel, llama, Angora goat, and Kashmir goat, may be bought from wool suppliers. Most of these wools come prepared for spinning, usually clean and well carded.

If you should obtain some of these fibers in the natural state (as some spinners do through arrangements with zoos), clean, oil, tease, and card them as you would wool. For fibers that are quite long and require worsted spinning, make the rolag by rolling up the carded wool across the width of the carder, laying the fibers parallel to each other.

Angora rabbit fur, which you may buy through the National Angora Rabbit Breeders Club, may be spun uncarded if it is plucked neatly and kept separated by layers of tissue paper until spun. A finer thread can be spun if the angora is very lightly teased and carded. When angora is to be spun in combination with wool, it is added to the wool during carding to mix the fibers.

Angora fur is very light and delicate, requiring careful handling at the spinning wheel to get exactly the right amount of twist, enough for strength but not so much that its softness is lost. It is necessary to make short, quick drafts, hands close together, to spin a fine yarn of the smooth, short fibers. There is no oil in Angora rabbit fur, so you may add some during spinning.

BLACK SHEEP

The fleece of black sheep is highly prized by handspinners. Black sheep are comparatively rare, because wool producers must cull out this rogue of the flock lest his fleece spoil the whole wool bag. The woolgrower is docked for black fleece, receiving less for it than for a comparable grade of white fleece. Handspinners, however, pay dearly for the black fleece from "Jacob's flock" when and *if* they can buy it.

Black fleece is not always black. It is any fleece that is not white, ranging from jet black through browns, tans, grays, and white fleeces with some black in them. Black lambs are born black but lighten after the first year, becoming lighter in color each year, shading into beautiful natural tones to which dyed colors cannot be compared. Natural dark fleeces do not fade, and the undyed shades blend harmoniously with each other.

Your chances of being able to get black fleece are, literally, one in a thousand sheep. There are a few suppliers who have black fleece from time to time. See "Helpful Information." Or you might have an interesting time hunting your own black sheep. For a beginning, try an ad in the farmers' classified section of a newspaper in your area or in one where sheep are raised.

Black fleece is spun like regular fleece. Special care should be used in sorting the fleece because there are subtle shadings of color within every dark fleece that could be overlooked in haste. For unique yarns, separate these shades to blend during carding with creamy white wool.

The dark fleece of Karakul sheep is also available from suppliers. It is long, coarse, curly, and interesting to spin.

JACOB'S FLOCK

All the sheep in Jacob's flock were "black sheep."

Let me pass through all your flock today, removing from it every speckled and spotted sheep and every black lamb, . . . and such shall be my wages.

—Jacob to Laban, Genesis XXX:32

Thus selection in sheep breeding began in Biblical times, and eventually black sheep, the rogues of the flock, became the connotation for all rascals. Now all black sheep belong to Jacob's flock.

SILK

Silk thread can be spun on a spinning wheel or with a small hand spindle, but cocoons or reeled silk filament, prepared for spinning, are almost impossible for the hobbyist to obtain from regular sources. Very little silk is produced in the United States today although there have been numerous enthusiastic and fairly successful efforts to establish sericulture since Colonial days. Mulberry trees, descendants of the white mulberries planted to feed silkworms, continue to prosper in localities where the silkworm craze abounded. At Pleasant Hill, Kentucky, near my home, where Shakers produced silk during the settlement's heyday, hearty red mulberry trees grow along village walks and provide fruit for a delicious berry cobbler served in the Shaker village dining room. Silk thread that the industrious sisters spun and silk fabrics they wove are on exhibit in the center family house, reminders that silk of high quality was a valued product in our area only a few pages back in its history.

Preparation of the filament from silk cocoons, even if they were available, is a highly specialized skill, not for amateurs. This interesting process of silk reeling may be seen at Greenfield Village in Dearborn, Michigan.

Interested (and indefatigable!) persons will, of course, write at once for the list of addresses offered by Newburgh Country Store and begin tracking down sources of silkworm eggs, cocoons, and silk waste that are sometimes available for experimental purposes, spinning, and exhibits. See "Helpful Information."

COTTON

In the bygone age of homespun, a shirt of sheer, well-spun cotton was a fine possession, more dear than one of soft wool or fine linen. Cotton grew best in the South, so the fiber had to be brought into other areas—no simple task in those days. Wherever the growing season was long enough, farmers tended their own small patches of cotton so that their wives could have the luxury of cotton fabrics.

Cotton was spun by hand on the flax wheel or the big wool wheel until Eli Whitney's cotton gin made home spinning impractical. Home spinning of cotton is still somewhat impractical, but the spinner who lives near areas where cotton is grown will find it interesting to do experimental cotton spinning, perhaps for educational or special projects.

The short, smooth cotton fibers are spun like other short fibers, such as Angora rabbit fur or short-staple wools. Pull the cotton fibers away from the seeds by hand. Cotton may be carded on fine cotton cards or "willowed" into a fluffy mass by beating it with a flexible twig. Because the cotton fibers are so short—from one-half inch to over an inch long, it can be spun into a very fine yarn when the spinner becomes adept at handling cotton. The spinning wheel must be treadled slowly, a short draw is used, and the tension is loosened to slow the rate of wind-on. A firm, short twist is needed, so the driving band is put into the warp (deeper) groove of the spindle pulley, as for woolen spinning.

There are not many fast dyes for cotton to be found in woods and meadows. Cotton does not take dye as easily as wool, and colors that are fast on wool are often fugitive on cotton. Old-time dyers favored copperas, indigo, and madder for cotton. Good results can also be expected from maple bark, hickory, and the ever-useful butternut dye.

QIVIUT, GOLDEN FLEECE OF THE ARCTIC

Someday the golden fleece of the Arctic, *qiviut*, the soft underfleece of the musk ox, will be plentiful enough to supply the need of handspinners. Due to the efforts of an ecologist, Dr. John J. Teal, Jr., the vanishing musk ox has been brought into captivity and successfully domesticated at the University of Alaska. This idealistic project, in its second decade of progress, aims not only to save musk oxen from threatened extinction but to aid needy peoples of the North by making it possible for them to harvest the valuable *qiviut* which has, for centuries, blown about and wasted on the barren Arctic tundras where *oomingmak*, the bearded one, grazes peacefully on willow shoots and grasses. Eskimo women are being taught to spin the *qiviut* and knit the yarn, soft as eiderdown and stronger than cashmere, into scarves and sweaters, which are sold to tourists and in fashionable shops. When the still-limited supply of *qiviut* becomes more plentiful, as musk ox herds increase on the farms of villagers along the northern coasts of North America, handspinners may at last be able to buy the rare golden fleece of the Arctic for their own spinning.

CHAPTER TEN

Plying and Skeining

When heavier yarn of more than a single strand is needed for strength or warmth, or simply for interest in texture and design, one strand of yarn may be twisted with another strand. This procedure is called plying. Two strands are the usual number plied together, but more may be used. The number of single yarns plied together is designated 2-ply, 3-ply, 4-ply, and so on.

Plying Yarns

Plying is usually done on a spinning wheel, with the two strands of yarn being spun together while the wheel turns in the direction opposite to the direction it turned during spinning. Spinning is done with the wheel turning clockwise, producing a left, or Z-twisted, yarn. Plying is done with the wheel turning counterclockwise, making yarn with a right, or S-twist (page 133). This is the usual rule, but not the

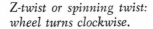

Z-twist or spinning twist:
wheel turns clockwise.

S-twist or plying twist:
wheel turns counter-clockwise.

only one. Plying is varied in all sorts of ways to make fancy or complicated yarns. For example, two Z-twisted strands plied by a Z-twist make a harder yarn than regular plying, because the twist is intensified by the twist on twist made by plying with the wheel turning in the same direction in which it turned when the yarn was spun. Or a Z-twisted single yarn may be plied by a Z-twist with an S-twisted single yarn, adding twist to one of the singles while reducing it in the other. There are many plying possibilities.

The full bobbins holding the yarns to be plied together are put onto a spool holder, which keeps the single strands of yarn from tangling as the bobbins unwind during plying. There may be a spool rack on your spinning wheel, as there is on my new parlor-type wheel bought in Canada. You could put the yarn, in balls, in two jam jars on the floor at your left, or even inside two paper bags. You could buy a "lazy Kate" bobbin holder or make one.

To make a bobbin holder, take a wooden or cardboard box wide enough to hold two bobbins (or three, or four) and bore holes in two sides of the box. Run a metal rod or a knitting needle through the holes, skewering the bobbins side by side on the shaft. Place the box on the floor at your left when you ply.

Tie the ends of the yarns to be plied together to the end of the spun yarn (the leader) left on the empty bobbin to facilitate beginning. Turn the wheel counterclockwise for plying and begin treadling slowly.

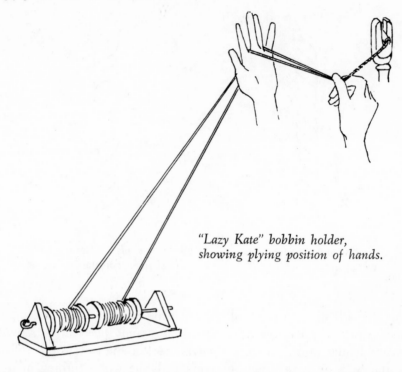

"Lazy Kate" bobbin holder,
showing plying position of hands.

Draw the yarns to be plied up from the bobbin rack through the fingers of the left hand, arranging the yarns so that each of them slips through different fingers. Guide the twisting yarns into the flyer with the right hand, holding back the yarn only enough to allow the desired amount of twist to form in the plied yarn. Plying can be done with loose or firm twist, according to your preference.

Woolen yarns are often plied, especially for knitting. Linen threads are not usually plied.

In the days when spinning was a regular part of the domestic routine, particular spinners had a special wheel for plying, because they felt plying on their spinning wheels got them out of kilter.

SKEINING YARNS

When finished, spun or plied yarn is wound off the spinning wheel onto a skeining device such as a niddy noddy, reel, or swift. The yarn is measured off into knots of 80 yards and skeins of 560 yards. A knot is tied in the yarn after each 80-yard length, which is 40 turns on a reel or niddy noddy measuring 2 yards around. There are 7 knots in a skein. The skein is also called a "hank" of yarn. Old-time mountain weavers used to say it was a "yard" because the skein of yarn was supposed to fill a yard of cloth.

Most skeining reels measure 2 yards around, but there are variations of an inch or two when you compare measurements of only a few of the old ones. Since even so slight a difference adds up to several yards, you can see why the skein was sometimes a half-pound of yarn rather than a certain yardage. The differences in sizes of reels and the tendency to err in counting the rounds resulted in development of the clock (or click) reel on which spinners in some areas were required to measure their skeins.

The clock reel (see below) counts its own revolutions on a wooden cog mechanism inside the reel support and announces the end of a knot of yarn with a loud click. Sometimes there is a dial and pointer, like a clock face, which keep track of the number of turns. Most clock reels measure 2 yards around, and 40 strands of yarn make the knot. The reel has four or six arms. The end of one arm lacks a raised edge,

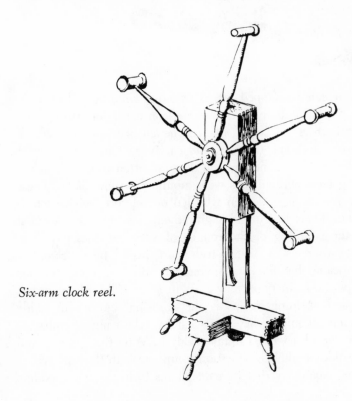

Six-arm clock reel.

Primitive skeining reel, now prized by collectors.

so that the yarn can be slipped off easily after winding. Clock reels are handsome pieces, with the reel mounted on a support rising from a low three- or four-legged bench, like the bench of a spinning wheel. Many reels have handsome turnings and carvings. Some are made of fine woods. The maker's name and the date are often inscribed on the bench. Skeining reels without legs were mounted on low bases. These are more primitive in design, often whittled out of soft woods such as poplar and pine. Their irregularities give them lots of charm, even if one must do the counting of the rounds of yarn for oneself. These roughly made yarn reels, or "wrap reels," are prized by collectors of primitive Americana, but today's spinner can still find them for sale in antique shops and at auctions. The clock reels are still fairly plentiful.

The simplest skeining device is the amusing and useful niddy noddy. Its whimsical appeal lies in its catchy folk name, familiar to many who have no idea what a niddy noddy is. Why this quaint hand reel is called a niddy noddy is a question to titillate both the antiquarian and the spinner. Some say that its name stems from the odd, nodding motion used to wind yarn with a niddy noddy. Another explanation is that since the job of skeining yarn often fell to an elderly granny who was known as a "niddy," the combination of her name with the nodding motions used in winding the yarn led to the name "niddy noddy." Or would you prefer "An old niddy nodding off for her forty winks while at her task of winding yarn"? Or, perhaps, "niddy" plus "knotty," for the knots she wound on the hand reel; or even "knit-ty" plus "knot-ty," which became niddy noddy for the sake of a rhythmic name to recite in the rhyme that was sung while winding yarn to help keep count of the rounds.

> Niddy noddy, niddy noddy,
> Two heads, one body,
> Here's one, 'Tain't one,
> 'Twill be one, bye and bye.
> Here's two, 'tain't two,
> 'Twill be two, bye and bye. (etc.)

When the verse reached the number forty, the knot was made. The

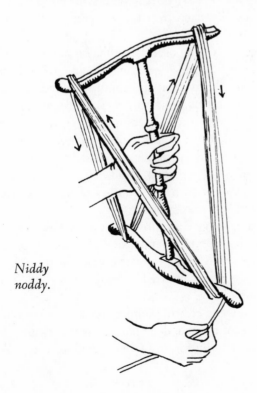

Niddy noddy.

"Song of the Niddy Noddy" also provided a riddle that was posed in every pioneer farmhouse where the niddy noddy was a common domestic item: "What has two heads, one body?" The answer, in singsong rhyme, was of course, "Niddy noddy, two heads, one body!"

An old niddy noddy, with well-turned center post and two graceful limbs set at odd angles, bespeaks the care taken by family craftsmen to make even the plainest household tools beautiful as well as useful. One of the two curving wooden limbs extending from the center post lacks a rim. To this limb the end of the yarn to be skeined off of the spinning wheel is tied. The yarn passes from one limb to the next, forming two large Vs. The niddy noddy is rocked back and forth, with the left hand grasping the center post while the yarn is wound over and under with the right hand. One complete round of the niddy noddy usually measures 2 yards, and forty rounds make the knot of yarn. The measurement of the old handmade niddy noddies varies widely, though, as did the measurement of spinners' skeins.

When the knot is made, the beginning and ending are tied together. An entire skein of yarn cannot be wound evenly on the niddy noddy. Tie the finished knot of yarn loosely with cotton cord in four places before removing the skein over the flat edge of one limb. Make the skein ties in a figure 8.

A swift, that handy folding accessory that fastens to a table's edge and is used by knitters to hold yarn skeins being wound into balls, can be used for making skeins from the spinning wheel too, though it serves less well than the others. The yarn is wound around the middle of the umbrella swift (page 139). Measure the circumference of the expanded swift to calculate the number of rounds equal to a knot of yarn. New swifts are available in most yarn and knitting shops. Some interesting old ones made of scrimshaw and carved woods can be seen in museums. Few old ones turn up in the collector's usual haunts, because the fragile strips break easily.

Some old spinning wheels of unique designs have yarn winders built onto them so that spinning and skeining can be done on one machine. Some of the old wool wheels have holes in the spokes of the large wheel where pegs were inserted to make a reel for unwinding the yarn from the spindle.

Lacking any of the described skeining devices, you could resort, temporarily, to the legs of an upended chair or someone's upheld hands. As neither serves satisfactorily for any length of time, you will want to

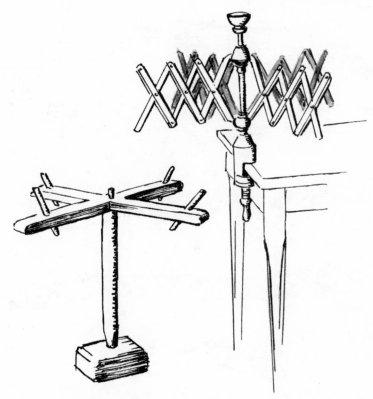

Old-time winding blades (left) and swift (right).

hunt for an old winding reel or inquire about a new niddy noddy or swift from the sources listed in the back of this book.

SETTING THE TWIST

Yarn can be left on the niddy noddy or reel for a time if it isn't needed at once for more reeling. Leaving the yarn like this, under tension, stretches it and helps remove the kinks, or overtwist. Then, when the yarn is removed from the reel, give it a light washing, or at least wet it, to set the twist firmly. If the yarn is very kinky, weight the lower loop of the hanging skein while it dries with a stone, heavy fishing weight, or other object that provides the right tension. See Chapter 5 for washing instructions.

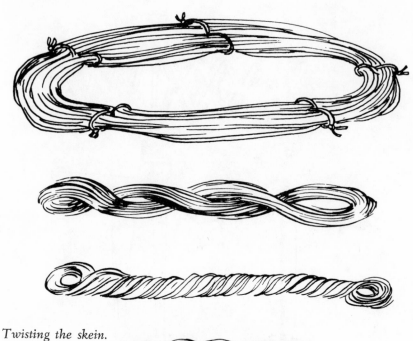

Twisting the skein.

TWISTING THE SKEIN

When the skein is finished, slip your hands inside it, stretch it between them, twist it until only a small loop is left at each end. Double the skein, tuck one loop through the other, and the skein is twisted.

Leave the yarn in the twisted skein until it is used. Wool kept in tightly wound balls for any length of time loses elasticity. When it is mordanted, washed, or dyed, the skein is untwisted, but left tied with the cotton cords to prevent tangling.

CHAPTER ELEVEN

The Delights
of Vegetable Dyeing

The delights of vegetable dyeing are unending. First, there is the beauty of its results—soft, glowing colors that blend as naturally as colors blend in nature; one-of-a-kind tones and hues that suit the originality of handspun yarns; rich, enduring shades of color that grow lovelier with fading and passage of time.

Aside from the unique dyes that are possible with natural dye-stuffs, there are other pleasures and surprises in the creation of colors that are deeply satisfying to the craftsman who spins yarn. Spinning and dyeing are basic companion crafts that act as steppingstones to each other as well as to other crafts. Handspun yarn creates the need for hand-dyed colors. Then, invariably, the colored handspun yarn creates the need for design. Thus the craftsman is led from spinning to dyeing to weaving, or knitting, or macramé, or stitchery, or crocheting, or to all of these. And what gives a craftsman more pleasure than the introduction to an untried craft?

Then there is the incidental pleasure of going afield to gather the natural dyestuffs. Pleasant mornings fly by as the search for dye plants leads one hither and yon, from flower to flower, from weeds to grasses, across woodland and meadow. The countryside takes on an inner dimension as the basket fills with stuff for the dye pot. Within the beauty of a blossom is the subtler tone of its dye color. Bright surprises wait in lowly weeds. Even dull leaves and ordinary grasses challenge the imagination. Nothing escapes the scrutiny of keen eyes in search of dyestuffs. The questing craftsman really *sees* what is around him.

The very awareness one brings to the meadow is a reward in itself. Eyes that see the obscure weed see, too, the secreted meadowlark's nest, the host of migratory monarch butterflies fluttering southward, the high-hanging hornet's nest among a tree's branches. These secrets of the meadow, which reveal themselves when the senses are attuned, are intimately bound up with the pleasures of creating dyes.

But the ultimate reward of going afield to gather dyestuffs is the color one extracts from the natural materials. The countryside is an endless palette of dyer's colors. There is pokeberry for red, sumac for gray, goldenrod for myriad hues of yellow, wild grapes for lavender, sassafras for tan, cocklebur for chartreuse, coreopsis for burnt orange, walnut hulls and lichens for browns—the possibilities are multitudinous.

The very fact that so many colors are there in the fields, waiting for the dye pot to reveal them, results in the dyer's greatest delight—the pleasure of experimenting with plants to make still another tone of a color, to perfect the dyeing technique, to discover a combination of dye plants leading to the "difficult" shades. For, while nature has been most lavish with shades of yellow in dye-yielding plants, and generous with browns, rust, tans, orange, rose, reddish-purple, gray, brownish-green, and greenish-yellow, there are colors that are difficult to obtain from common natural dyestuffs. To create the bright green, clear red, deep purple, jet black, and strong blue is the dyer's greatest challenge.

To obtain the difficult colors without the help of synthetic dyes, the vegetable-dyeing enthusiast must add to her store of natural materials from surrounding fields and woods the rarer, ancient dye plants from commercial supply houses. Madder root gives the rich red color cherished by dyers throughout the ages, considered choice by antiquarians of today who prize the enduring, mellowed tones of madder in old handwoven coverlets. Indigo is a dye name synonymous with deep, clear blue since Europe's sixteenth century. There is logwood for purple and for darkest black and the tropical insect cochineal for the brilliant scarlet or a purple color, depending on the method of dyeing. To obtain the difficult true green, a good yellow must be top-dyed with a good blue—indigo. Goldenrod can provide a clear yellow, but for the true blue there is no alternative for the "blue pot" made with indigo.

And so the search for natural colors leads the dyer on. The yen for quantities of hard-to-get herbs, blossoms, and rare dyestuffs brings the dyer to growing dye plants for himself. A dye garden is fascinating, colorful, and fragrant. All the plants grown in it yield dye—herbs, flowers, wild plants brought in from the countryside, and rare dye plants such as woad and madder. Colonial ladies who prized color in their household linens found dye plants as necessary in their gardens as vegetables or medicinal and culinary herbs. Contemporary dyers, too, are discovering for themselves the pleasures of a dye garden.

But where does the craftsman living in today's compactly designed home store and use the color-filled harvest of countryside and dye garden? Soon the increasing store of materials and accessories of dyeing demand their own space in our houses. There may be a corner of a dry, warm attic, basement, garage, utility room, or porch where the dyer's art may prosper. Ideally there is an entire room that serves as the dye shed. The main advantage of a dye shed, used exclusively for dyeing (or for spinning and dyeing), is that the "mess" is taken out of the living area of the house. There is no need to keep the dyeing accouterments put away between projects for neatness' sake. There is plenty of room to keep such things as weeds, tree bark, and nut hulls, which are far too messy to bring inside the house. A spilled kettle or a colorful stain on the floor doesn't matter in the dye shed. Dye cauldrons can boil and bubble with never a worry about clearing off the burners when it's time to prepare dinner. Even the most tolerant family will rejoice when dyeing is done in the dye shed instead of the kitchen.

The dye shed is a fascinating place. Overhead beams are hung with fragrant sheaves of drying herbs and grasses. Baskets with intriguing contents stand on the floor and tables. Wooden bowls and firkins are filled to overflowing with oak galls, nut hulls, lichens, and blossom heads. Spicy aromas rise on clouds of steam above a deep kettle on top of the small black wood stove. Skeins of dyed yarn in soft mellow colors hang in colorful loops along a wall on Shaker pin boards. On the cupboard shelf, glass canisters hold powders and crystals labeled with chemical names such as copperas, stannous chloride, and potassium bitartrate. On the table wooden dye sticks, spoons, and spacious enamel dye pots are in readiness. And in the big splint basket is a great mound of uncarded wool waiting to receive color.

The dye shed.

Before the wool will take dye properly it must be mordanted. The mordant binds the dye to the wool fibers. Without a mordant bath most dye colors are not permanent and fade in sunlight and water. The mordant makes colors fast. Derived from the Latin word *mordere,* which means "to bite," a mordant means any caustic substance that fixes a dye color. Some common mordants the dyer uses are tin crystals, chrome, iron, alum, vinegar, oak bark, plant galls, cream of tartar, lime, ammonia, caustic soda, and blue vitriol.

Mordants affect the color produced by a dyestuff too. Each mordant produces a different color or toning of a color when used with a particular dyestuff. Sassafras, for example, gives pinkish brown with chrome mordant, brown with alum, and gray when copperas is used. Use of mordants makes possible a wider range of colors and enriches their tones.

Dyeing is an experimental art. There are recipes, rules, and formulas to follow, but there are always unpredictable elements that affect the dyer's art. Fleece from two different sheep dyed in the same vat will come out with detectable differences in coloring. Barks and roots of trees make different shades of a color in spring and autumn, with autumn colors usually being the stronger. Mature plants generally make deeper colors than young ones. Fresh materials give colors unlike those of dried dyestuffs. Subtle differences in shading of colors can even be attributed to the soil in which a dye plant grows. The dyer can control the color she creates only to a certain point. From then on these variables in the dyestuffs take over and contribute surprises that never fail to delight the craftsman when the colored wool lifts from the dye pot.

There are other intangibles in the making of natural dyes which affect the colors in ways we cannot see. What brown has such delicate nuances of shading as brown from walnut hulls picked up under a tree while a red squirrel scolds overhead? Is there a prettier, more poignant shade of yellow than yellow given by goldenrods that bloom everywhere in an August countryside, tinting whole fields golden and calling up the beloved image of Grandfather, who sneezed sneeze after sneeze over goldenrod? These are the associations we form that give the subtle, underlying tones of meaning to dyes we create from natural dyestuffs gleaned from woodland and meadow.

BASIC PROCEDURES

Handling wool: Wool is a strong, absorbent, soft, warm, resilient, attractive fiber. Improper handling of fleece, yarn, or fabric destroys or reduces these qualities. Wool must be handled carefully to prevent damage.

Do not plunge wool into hot water. High temperatures cause shrinking, matting, and hardening of its fibers. Begin with cool or lukewarm water and increase temperatures gradually. Do not allow wool to change temperature suddenly, either going from cold to hot or from hot to cold. A lukewarm temperature (98° F.–100° F.) is safest for wool, but it withstands higher temperatures if brought to them gradually. Wool may be heated to the simmering point (190° F.–210° F.) and held there without damage. *Never* boil wool.

"Mind you don't harass the wool," Grandmother cautioned when we washed the skeins of wool in her deep washtubs there by the well under the shade of the grape arbor. Wool needs gentle treatment when it is wet. Too much stirring around during washing, mordanting, or dyeing causes matting and shrinking. Move the wool back and forth gently or up and down under the surface of the water, never around and around.

Do not hold wool out of the water while it is saturated and weighted with the water. Wool absorbs more than half its weight in water; when it is saturated, the fibers weaken and stretch. This may cause a knitted garment to lose shape. Squeeze the excess water from the skein, fleece, or fabric as it is lifted up out of the water, or, if it is hot, lift it out of the water into an enameled colander, where it can drain until cool enough to be squeezed with the hands.

Do not wring or twist wool to extract moisture. Squeeze or press it with the hands. For large quantities an old-fashioned hand-turned washday "wringer" is handy, or an old-time "washday's helper," the wooden crossed-paddle gadget that served well to agitate clothes in the washtub when such things were done the hard way.

DYEING

Before dyeing: Weigh the wool to be dyed while it is dry and before mordanting. Wool may be dyed in the fleece, skein, or fabric. Skeins must be loosely tied with cotton string, not wool yarn, which stretches. The goods to be dyed must be clean, free of grease, and thoroughly wet.

Wetting goods before dyeing or mordanting: Wool, or other goods, must be thoroughly wet before entering mordant or dye bath. Moisture opens the outer scaly layer of wool fibers and swells the inner layer of fibers, letting dye or mordant penetrate well.

When wool is washed just before mordanting and dyeing are begun, let the scoured wool lie in the last rinse water until time to enter the mordant, then leave it in the mordant until the dye bath is ready.

If the wool was scoured and mordanted, then dried and laid aside for a time, immerse it in clear water while the dye bath is prepared. Press out excess moisture before entering wetted wool into dye bath.

The dye bath: For each pound of wool, use a dye bath of 4 gallons, or slightly more, made of soft, lukewarm water and the dye extract. The dye extract is made by boiling the prepared plant parts for a specified time, then straining the dye ooze into soft water in the proper dye pot.

Enter the clean wetted wool into the dye bath while the bath is lukewarm (98° F.–100° F.), then heat to the simmering point (190° F.–210° F.) and hold at that temperature as long as directions specify. Move the wool gently during the process and keep it under the dye. If the dye bath evaporates, lift the wool out, add hot water to bring the bath back to the original amount, mix well, and return the wool to the dye pot. Always remove the wool when any substance is added to the dye bath during dyeing or uneven dyeing may result.

Never boil the wool, and handle it carefully while it is wet, to avoid damage to the fibers.

As long as there is color in the dye bath, it may be used again to dye more wool, but each new batch will dye lighter than the last.

Dye enough wool at once for whatever use it is intended. You cannot dye precisely the same shade twice, although you might come close enough to blend the fibers during carding. Colors made with natural dyes will always harmonize, however great the variation in shade.

To rinse and dry goods after a dye bath: The dyed goods is lifted from the simmering dye bath into the first rinse water in an enameled pail, the temperature of which is almost as hot as the dye bath. Clear, soft water must be used for rinsing, as for dyeing. The second rinse is a bit cooler than the first rinse, the third rinse is still cooler. Rinsing and gradual cooling continues thus until the last rinse is clear. Do not wring or twist the wool during rinsing. Do not lift a skein of wool out of the water and hold it up while weighted with water; keep the wool under the water during rinsing, dunking it gently beneath the surface of the water. When rinsing is complete, squeeze out excess moisture by hand, then roll the goods in a towel to absorb more moisture. Spread fleece on a drying rack or hang skeins of wool in the shade to dry, except when directions for dyeing call for sunshine-dried wool.

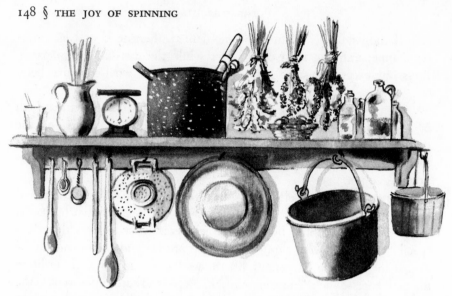

Dyeing equipment: dye pot, dye sticks, cooking thermometer, heatproof glass measures, plastic measuring spoons, rinse buckets, scales.

The dye pot must be large enough to hold, without crowding, 4 gallons of dye solution and one pound of wool. Unless otherwise specified in the directions for dyeing, the dye pot should be of stainless steel or enamel or graniteware with no chips or cracks. Metals act as mordants, and chips that expose the metal underneath the coating allow the metal of the container to enter into the dyeing process. If the dyer is striving for a particular color, the accidental use of an unexpected mordant will make a color other than the one intended.

Other recipes for natural dyes call for use of an iron dye pot to "sadden" the color. In pioneer days that all-purpose hearthside vessel, the black iron kettle, was used for everything—cooking, washing, lye making, lard rendering, candle making, dyeing, and the like. The simple dyes that colored the rough homespun fabrics were brewed either in a small pot that hung on a trammel inside the fireplace or in a fat, blackened cauldron suspended from a log tripod over a wood fire outside in the cabin dooryard.

An outdoor arrangement such as the pioneer's log tripod or an outdoor fireplace is splendid for brewing dyes that give off strong odors, or simply when one would enjoy more being outside while the task is done.

Many dyers use a brass kettle or a copper wash boiler, as I do, for dyeing colors that are helped by these mordants. The copper wash boiler is made to order for the top of the two-burner laundry stove in my dye shed. And what is more handsome than a shining brass kettle on a pothook in the fireplace? Hooray for the dyer who rescues such bygones as wash boilers, iron cauldrons, and brass kettles from the fate of serving as flower pots and magazine holders and puts them back where they belong—over fires, with contents steaming.

To stir the yarn in the dye bath the dyer needs a painted wooden dye stick that will not stain in the dye, or several unpainted sticks, one for each color. Use your ingenuity here—wooden dowels, long-handled wooden spoons, discarded drumsticks, broom handles, or whatever.

A thermometer is a necessity if the heat of the dye bath is to be accurately controlled. Use a regular cooking thermometer.

Heatproof glass measuring pitchers should be used when liquids are measured. Pint and quart sizes are practical.

Nonmetal spoons, plastic or wood, should be used for measuring and stirring. Both mordants and metals are chemicals, so the right combinations can cause minor chemical reactions resulting in corrosion of the spoons, for example, or alteration of color results. Dye stains clean easily from plastic too.

The rinse buckets should be enamelware or plastic for ease in handling and cleaning. Enamelware or plastic washbasins or dishpans serve well too.

For weighing out the pound of wool or yarn to be dyed and the correct amount of dyestuff, a pair of scales is necessary. I tie bulky materials in a mesh laundry bag and weigh them on a brass hanging scale. An ordinary kitchen scale is perfect for weighing smaller amounts of dyestuff or mordant.

These are the basic items needed for dyeing. Nevertheless you will soon collect more dyeing equipment than I describe. At once you begin to discover clever dyeing uses for items about the house, and, before long, the enameled colander, the slotted spoon, the tea strainer, the plastic pitcher, the postal scale are spirited from kitchen to dye shed.

Has anyone seen the brandy jigger?

MORDANTS

Mordants are chemicals that unite with the dye in the fibers to enrich the color and make it permanent. Mordants are applied to the fiber before, during, or after the dye bath, depending on the dye and the fiber being dyed.

Mordanting must be done carefully on clean, grease-free materials or the dye will streak or fade. When the mordant penetrates the fibers and is held by them, the color is clear and fast. Animal fibers (wool and silk) absorb mordant better than vegetable fibers (cotton and linen); thus dyes that are permanent on wool and silk may be fugitive on cotton or linen. Because wool is the easiest fiber to dye and to spin, and because of its natural qualities and availability, the directions given here for mordanting and dyeing are for one pound of wool.

DIRECTIONS FOR MORDANTING

ALUM MORDANT

Alum or potash alum (potassium aluminum sulfate) was the favorite mordant of old-time dyers. Buy this today at the drugstore. Alum used for pickling, available in groceries, is ammonium alum, less successful for mordanting than potash alum. Too much alum leaves wool sticky. Very fine wool requires less alum and shorter time in the mordant bath.

Prepare a water bath of 4 gallons of soft, lukewarm water in an enamelware kettle. Dissolve 3 ounces of alum and 1 ounce of cream of tartar and add to the water bath. Immerse the clean, wetted wool in the mordant bath and heat gradually to simmering. Hold at simmering (*never boil*) for an hour, gently spreading and stirring the wool with a nonmetal stirrer. Remove from the heat and allow wool to cool in the mordant, or leave overnight. Remove wool from the mordant bath, squeeze the moisture out, and transfer at once to the dye bath, or dry for later dyeing. Rinse only if the wool feels sticky.

CHROME MORDANT

Chrome (potassium dichromate) is a fine mordant for wool which gives brighter, stronger, clearer colors than alum. It must be handled carefully because it is very sensitive to light and exposure leaves streaks in the product. *Caution: chrome is harmful if swallowed or inhaled.*

Prepare a water bath of 4 gallons of soft, lukewarm water in an enamelware kettle. Dissolve ½ ounce of chrome in hot water and add it to the water bath. Enter the clean wetted wool. Cover the kettle at once with a plate, which will keep the wool under the water to prevent uneven dyeing. Bring the mordant bath to simmering and hold at that temperature for an hour, turning the wool once or twice with a non-metal stirrer. Rest the wool in the mordant until cool enough to handle, then rinse in water of the same temperature as the mordant bath. Squeeze out the rinse water and transfer the mordanted wool at once to a dye bath of the same temperature as the rinse water. If there is a delay between rinsing and immersion in the dye bath, keep the wool covered and protected from the light.

GOLDENROD (*Solidago*)

Goldenrod, the graceful flower of sunlit autumn fields and road-sides in most of the United States, gives a wide range of yellows for the dye pot. The flower heads, fluffy sprays of tiny golden florets, are best for dyeing when picked as they come into bloom and when used fresh. The mordant determines the shade of yellow goldenrod gives.

To prepare dye: Cover 1 peck (or more) of goldenrod flowers with cold water and bring to a boil. Boil for one hour or longer to extract color from flowers. Strain dye extract into a dye pot that con-tains additional lukewarm water to make a 4-gallon dye bath.

To dye Grandmother's Goldenrod Yellow: Mordant one pound of wool with 4 ounces of alum and 1 ounce of cream of tartar in 4 gallons of water. (See p. 150.) Submerge the wet wool in a dye bath prepared as directed above and simmer for about 30 minutes, stirring often and gently. When the color suits, rinse the goods in several waters until the water stays clear, with the temperature of the first rinse being about the same as the dye bath, then each successive rinse a bit cooler. Press water out of the wool and dry in the sun.

To dye yellowish-tan: Enter one pound of alum-mordanted wet wool (see p. 150) into a lukewarm goldenrod dye bath prepared as above. Keep the dye bath simmering for 30 minutes, with the goods submerged in the bath. Stir gently during dyeing. Then trans-fer the wool into a second bath that contains 1/6 ounce chrome and 1/6 ounce acetic acid (or 6-7 tablespoons vinegar). Stir gently while goods simmer for 15 minutes. Rinse in clear water, the first rinse being about the same temperature as the dye bath, the second a bit cooler, and so on. Squeeze out the excess water and hang the wool in the shade to dry.

To dye "brass": Mordant one pound of wool with chrome (see p. 150). Immediately immerse the wet goods in a lukewarm goldenrod dye bath. Heat bath to simmering and maintain the temperature for about 30 minutes. Keep the wool under the water at all times to prevent uneven dyeing. Rinse and dry, following basic procedure on page 147.

Sumac branch and berries.

SUMAC (*Rhus* genus)

The scarlet berries of the sumac bush, which are the source of the tangy wilderness beverage known as "Indian lemonade," make yellowish-tan and gray dyes. The feather-shaped leaves and young shoots of the sumac plant give shades of brown, from tan to dark brown. The entire cluster of hairy red berries is picked and used fresh in summertime for the strongest color, but may be dried to use later. The leaves and shoots are gathered in late summer and dried. Sumac berries contain malic acid, and the seeds, when boiled, release tannin; the leaves, too, contain tannin, so no mordant is necessary to get gray from the berries or browns from the leaves. Early settlers of America called scarlet sumac "diar's shumach," after a related species used in Europe.

To prepare dye from sumac berries: Crush ½ peck of red sumac berries. Soak at least 30 minutes or overnight, then boil 30 minutes to extract the color. Strain the liquid into a dye pot that contains enough lukewarm water to make a 4-gallon dye bath.

To dye yellowish-tan: Enter one pound of wet alum-mordanted wool (see p. 150) into a lukewarm sumac-berry dye bath prepared as above. Heat to simmering and process 45 minutes, stirring gently. Rinse and dry in the shade, following directions on page 147.

To dye gray: Add 1 teaspoon copperas to the lukewarm dye bath made with the strained dye ooze extracted from sumac berries. Enter one pound of wetted wool, *without mordanting,* into the warm dye bath and simmer 30 minutes. Rinse and dry in the shade, following the basic procedure on page 147.

To prepare dye from scarlet sumac leaves and shoots: Cut the dried leaves and shoots fine and soak overnight in water to cover. Next morning boil 30 minutes or more to extract dye. Strain the liquid into the dye pot with enough water to make a 4-gallon dye bath.

To dye shades of brown: Enter one pound of wetted wool, *without mordanting,* into a lukewarm dye bath containing an extract of sumac leaves and shoots. Heat to the simmering point and hold until the brown is as dark as desired. Rinse and dry according to the basic procedure on page 147.

POKEBERRIES

In late summer the home dyer visits the pokeweed patch as eagerly as the wild-foods enthusiast visits it in springtime. But now dark-purple berries hang in clusters along the coarse pokeweed stalks where, earlier, tender green leaves were taken for the springtime mess of greens. The shiny, scalloped berries of the pokeweed (*Phytolacca americana*) are the source of a lovely red dye that is similar to cochineal red. Pokeberry red fades with time but to a shade that has its own beauty.

To prepare pokeberry dye: Boil gently for 30 minutes or more ½ bushel of ripe pokeberries in water containing ½ gallon of vinegar. Strain and add to the dye extract the vinegar water in which the wool was mordanted and enough clear water to make a 4-gallon dye bath.

*Pokeweed sprouts
in the spring.*

*Branches with berries
in the autumn.*

To dye pokeberry red: Enter one pound of wet wool into a lukewarm pokeberry dye bath immediately after mordanting the wool in water containing ½ gallon of vinegar. Bring the bath to the simmering point and simmer for ½ hour or more until the desired color of red is reached. Keep the wool pressed under the water. Do not skimp on the amount of dyestuff: too light a red results from too few berries. Press the water from the dyed wool and hang it to dry without rinsing to further set the color. After a few days rinse the wool and dry again.

SASSAFRAS

Sassafras, that common roadside tree whose fiery leaves delight admirers of autumnal foliage, contributes rich color to the dye pot as well as to the landscape. But it is not from the many-shaped leaves (who can resist looking for a mitten shape?) that the best dye is obtained. The fragrant bark of the root gives rosy-tans and rosy-browns that are fairly fast and especially pleasing. The choice rosy colors come from roots dug in late summer and early fall.

To prepare sassafras dye: Soak in water overnight 1 peck of sassafras roots or 8 to 12 ounces of dry sassafras root bark. Next morning boil the root bark 30 minutes, the roots 2 hours, to extract the dye. Strain and add lukewarm water to make a 4-gallon dye bath.

To dye rose-tan: Enter one pound of alum-mordanted wetted wool into a lukewarm dye bath containing sassafras dye ooze and heat to the simmering point. Simmer for 30 minutes. Then, without rinsing, move the dyed wool to a mordant bath, of the same temperature as the dye bath, which contains 4 gallons of water and ½ ounce of copperas. Stir carefully and continue simmering for 10 minutes. Rinse and dry according to the basic procedure on page 147.

To dye rose-brown: Enter one pound of chrome-mordanted wetted wool into a lukewarm sassafras dye bath. Heat to the simmering point and maintain the temperature for 30 minutes, keeping wool moving gently. Rinse and dry (see page 147).

DYER'S BONUS: SASSAFRAS ROOT TEA

Dig some small sassafras roots in the springtime, the earlier the better, and scrub them clean. Cut the roots into lengths that fit into

Sassafras leaves and roots.

an enamelware kettle. Use a generous handful of roots to about 2 quarts of water. Bring the kettle to a boil, then simmer until the brew is a pretty, rosy color, about 10-15 minutes. Strain the tea, sweeten to taste with honey or sugar, and serve hot or iced. Add a slice of lemon if you prefer.

Many Hoosiers add sugar and milk to hot sassafras tea and call it "saloop."

The bark of sassafras root dug in the springtime may be peeled off and dried to use for sassafras tea all year long.

Margaret Reed of Beaver Falls, Pennsylvania, also uses the spicily scented greenish-yellow sassafras blossoms to make tea. "Get yourself some this spring," she wrote. "The tea has a better flavor. Most people never look for these delicious blossoms."

Black Walnut (*Juglans nigra*)

Black-walnut hulls give a rich dark brown that is fast without mordanting. Mordants are sometimes used to enrich or vary the colors, but a simple lasting dye is made without them. Walnut hulls are gathered and used green or dried for later use. Save green hulls to use later by covering them with water and storing them away in a dark place until needed. The longer the hulls soak, the darker the brown will be. Walnut hulls make a strong dye. One dye bath goes a long way, dyeing several pounds of wool. The first bath dyes dark brown and later ones dye lighter and lighter shades of brown as the color depletes. Black-walnut shells or bark, as well as hulls, are used for brown dye. The hulls of butternut, or white walnut (*Juglans cinerea*), also make a good, fast dye. During the American Civil War, Confederate soldiers became known as "butternuts" because this was the color of the stout homespun clothes worn by southern backwoods boys, who came, without uniforms, to fight beside Robert E. Lee. The homely color of butternut dyed in the wool is still a reminder of their tattered valor.

To prepare dye from walnut hulls: Soak ½ peck of walnut hulls (dried or fresh green hulls) in water overnight or longer. Boil them 2 hours or more. The longer the boiling, the darker the dye. Strain the ooze into enough water to make a 4-gallon dye bath.

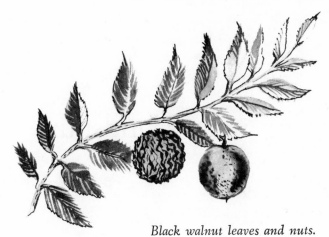

Black walnut leaves and nuts.

To dye walnut-hull brown: Enter the wetted wool into a lukewarm black-walnut dye bath *without mordanting*. Heat to the simmering point and simmer 30 minutes. Keep the wool under the water. Rinse and dry according to the basic procedure on page 147.

To darken ("sadden") the color, use an iron kettle for boiling the dye ooze and for the dye bath.

A mordant may be used to brighten and enrich the color. Alum-mordanted wool becomes a warm yellow-brown. Walnut hulls on chrome-mordanted wools dye a darker brown than wool without mordant. One tablespoon of copperas and a handful of sumac berries added to the dye bath make the brown almost black.

Butternut hulls make a softer shade of brown—tan on unmordanted wool and darker tan with 1 teaspoon of copperas added to the dye bath.

Dyer's Reading List

Adrosko, Rita J., *Natural Dyes in the United States.* Smithsonian Institution Press, Washington, D.C., 1968.

Davidson, Mary Frances, *The Dye-Pot.* Published by Author, Gatlinburg, Tennessee, 1950.

Lesch, Alma, *Vegetable Dyeing.* Watson Guptill Publications, New York, 1970.

———, *Dye Plants and Dyeing—A Handbook.* Brooklyn Botanic Garden, Brooklyn, New York, 1964.

CHAPTER TWELVE

Creating with Handspun

Needlework has long been a medium of expression for woman's creative impulse. The treasured examples of early American needlework, which are so carefully preserved in museums and private collections, reflect the artistry of women who, with inventive needle and handspun yarns, stitched the very design and pattern of their lives into their family's clothing and household linens. The whole scope of those bygone days is worked in stitch and pattern on homespun fabrics that were themselves the products of months of hard work.

These women commemorated their nation's birth and the new American spirit with eagle and stars in their needlework. They adapted Old World designs and symbols to fit their lives, making them freer and more spontaneous on spacious backgrounds, as their own lives had become. They abandoned old styles of needlework, replacing their stiff formality with vigorous designs flowing with the energy and growth of their surroundings—birds flying, flowers blooming, trees fruiting, grapes vining, ships sailing, horses running, deer leaping. In needlework that they believed was destined only for their own use, not for our museums,

Colonial women unwittingly made a pictorial history of their lives and times that we can understand today as clearly as though the stitches were words.

Even though museum needlework has a quality of anonymity about it because we do not know its maker, there is also a personal expression of the woman who made it in every piece of embroidery or needlepoint or weaving or hooking or appliqué or knitting or quilting. In careful stitches and glowing colors that woman outlined her love and thoughtfulness for her child, her husband, her friend, or her home. In her efforts to create an extra bit of beauty for their pleasure we see a measure of her unselfishness and devotion to their needs. We can guess what is meaningful to her by her designs—home, nature, children, church, country. We can see her fondness for color or flowers or stars or animals. We sense her spirit, marvel at her energy, admire her skill, judge her talent and originality. We know much about her, but we do not know her name. The aura of her personality is there for us to see in her needlework long after her identity is lost.

The graceful designs and patterns worked in handspun threads with practiced stitches were jubilant finishing touches on projects that took months in the making, beginning with woolshearing or pulling flax. Imagine the complete satisfaction those pleasurable stitches brought to women who, through need, were required to develop self-reliance and

Signed sampler.

skill enough to produce their own textiles, start to finish. Needlework was the joyful bonus, the colorful blessing, that lightened the burden of women's work.

Today's spinner, through choice, can indulge her own sense of beauty and savor the same satisfaction that comes of being able to provide for one's self and family, of being able to create with one's hands a useful and beautiful item. She can use her handspun yarns to create a piece of needlework, from start to finish, that will outlive its usefulness in her time, possibly to take its place in tomorrow's collections of twentieth-century American needlework.

Every piece of needlework has its own distinctive quality that links it to its maker as certainly as her fingerprints or handwriting. When we recognize this personal quality in work done by our friends and contemporaries today we say, "This looks like Ellen," or "Adele made this—she has a 'thing' about ancient symbols." The distillation of this individual quality, especially if it is quite original, unique, and pleasing, is the very quality that brings fame to artists, musicians, poets, or needleworkers. To those of us whom fame eludes, the recognizable personal quality in our work is simply a satisfying, albeit less eloquent, expression of ourselves. "This is mine," it says. "I made it myself."

Use your handspun yarns and threads for any of the traditional forms of needlework you enjoy. These are the same yarns and threads used by women two-hundred years ago when they created the fine early-American needlework and textiles we admire in museum collections. Your only limitation is your own skill. You must develop enough skill to produce the type of yarn or thread best suited for the needlework you intend to do. Everything else is much easier for us in these days of plenty than it was for the women who began the tradition of American needlework.

If you love the old patterns, designs, and techniques, you may wish to copy a favorite coverlet or a piece of crewel, being faithful to the last detail. Perhaps you will adapt the old designs, symbols, and stitches to suit yourself, as the Colonial ladies did when they changed the English Rose to the Wild Rose and the King's Crown to Potomac Pride. Or you may want to update the old designs by adding to them significant new symbols of our own historic times—spacecraft, the atom, the DNA molecule, or a peace symbol.

In addition to the traditional forms of needlework in which you may use your handspun there are contemporary forms of needlework for which handspun is especially suited, such as stitchery and woven

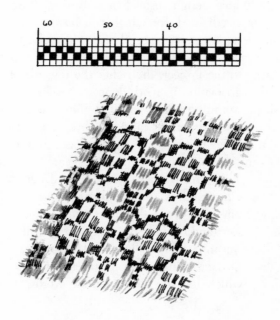

Yarns may be spun for a special purpose.

contemporary wall hangings. Traditional designs may be used or adapted for these or they may be worked in abstract designs.

Be sure to stitch your name and the date into any piece of needlework you create even though you (like the Colonial ladies) do not foresee your stitches in museums of the twenty-second century. This is especially important if you copy an old piece to the last detail. It is your duty to prevent incorrect dating being affixed to it, either by accident or intent, after it leaves your hands.

Chances are that today's spinner was led to the spinning wheel in the first place by another strong enthusiasm—weaving or dyeing or knitting or crewel work or stitchery—for which she needs handspun yarns to complete an ideal. The use for which she intends her yarn is foremost in her mind during its spinning.

Yarn spun for a special purpose takes on its character and meaning even before it is taken from the spindle. The plan for the tapestry or the sweater or the coverlet or the place mats dictates the type of fleece spun, the method of spinning, the type of twist, the smoothness or

162 § THE JOY OF SPINNING

irregularity, even the color of the dyes. Yarn spun to fit a specific need is part of the whole design instead of only a medium for the design.

A piece of needlework for which you have produced all the components—the design, the yarn or thread, the color, the fabric—is an ultimate in artistic expression. You may go even a step farther, for the more you bring to the project, the richer the rewards of enjoyment and the deeper the satisfaction in work done with your hands. Perhaps you will refinish the spinning wheel you use, grow the dye plants for coloring the yarn in your garden, or raise the sheep for the fleece.

When a spinner has seen the woolly fleece on the back of a sheep (her own!) running through the meadow, sheared it, carded the fleece, spun it, dyed it, then created from it a treasured item for her own use, or her friend's, or her family's, her delight in that yarn is a many-faceted joy. It springs from deep personal sources and cannot be fully described for another's understanding. This is truly the joy of spinning, which, like all of life's meaningful joys, you must experience for yourself in your own way. So take up the delicate thread of your own fascination with spinning, which led you to read these words, and follow it.

CHAPTER THIRTEEN

Following the Golden Thread

The whirr of a spinning wheel is music to the ear of the spinner. It is a tune as spellbinding as the sizzling of a green log on a cheery fire, as compelling as the Pied Piper's flute. Since that day in Gatlinburg when its familiar, heart-warming sound stirred up my slumbering fascination for spinning wheels, I have followed its lure from one corner of the country to another. Every business itinerary includes side trips to enable me to visit places in that area where spinning is done for public viewing or museums that house fine collections of spinning paraphernalia. Even family vacations are routed so that I may take in a nearby spinning workshop or craft fair.

Still, my husband and two sons are not vacation martyrs for the cause of Mom's spinning. Everyone enjoys having specific destinations along the roads we travel together and spinning points of interest have led all of us to memorable experiences. There is always something to entertain the rest of the family while I carry on my romance with spinning wheels. Sometimes the boys disappear to take a stagecoach ride around a restored village (or to eat a hamburger) while my husband goes off to watch other craftsmen working. Bob once caught a fine rainbow trout in a nearby stream while I sat under the blue-and-white-striped tent at a spinning seminar, and his brother Jim rode our host's Welsh ponies to his heart's content over the green hillsides of their Canadian farm. Once, when I enjoyed myself too much to take leave of an herb garden, lush with dye plants, my husband went up the road exploring and came back the owner of a Vermont mountain farm with its own waterfall. I ask you, how could my family become bored with indulging my fancy when they catch such splendid fish for themselves?

Our meandering journeys from restoration to craft fair, from workshop to museum, from sheep ranch to wool mill, have been rich experiences for me as a spinner. They have led me to other spinners and new friendships, to stores of information and new techniques. Trips in search of spinning were the wellsprings of enthusiasms that prompted me to write this book, winding up, like a ball of spun yarn, my own personal odyssey along the path of a golden thread spun out in my grandmother's kitchen.

Helpful Information

Wellsprings for Spinners

The new spinner learning to spin on her own, perhaps with the aid of this book, will want to see spinning demonstrated. It is often helpful just to watch someone else spinning with expertise. This may be all the beginner needs to smooth a rough spot in her spinning technique or to understand that baffling part on her spinning wheel.

There are many places where one may see spinners at work, either regularly or on special days. In fact, there are so many such places that I cannot list all of them here. Besides, finding out where spinning may be seen and visiting the location is an integral part of every spinner's own personal spinning adventure and often the way to a serendipitous discovery of one sort or another—you shall see! Following are some suggestions to begin with.

Obvious places where spinning is demonstrated are restored or re-created museum villages and historical cities, such as Colonial Williamsburg in Williamsburg, Virginia; Shakertown at Pleasant Hill, Kentucky;

Old Sturbridge Village in Sturbridge, Massachusetts; Old Salem in Winston-Salem, North Carolina; Conner Prairie Pioneer Settlement in Noblesville, Indiana; and many, many others. Such places present spinning in its authentic historical context. Also look for spinning when traveling in other countries—Canada, Scotland, New Zealand, South America, and so on. And don't forget historical homes and sites, folk art centers, state parks, and theme parks, such as Knott's Berry Farm's Ghost Town in Buena Park, California. Consult travel guide books, such as the Mobil Travel Guide for the United States; state and national tourism bureaus; the travel sections of newspapers and magazines; and the indispensible spinning periodicals (listed below). Following the trail of spinning might be the focus of a vacation or an interesting side trip when you are traveling about. You will certainly be led to fascinating destinations you might otherwise have missed.

Spinning in the contemporary mode may often be seen at the ubiquitous craft fairs in summer and autumn. These may be local affairs held at varying times, but some are large established events that are held year after year, such as the Southern Highland Handicraft Guild Craftsman's Fairs held in Asheville, North Carolina, every July and October. County and state fairs are also good places to see spinning, with "Sheep to Shawl" events being highlights at various fairs. These are lively competitive events for spinners' and weavers' guilds that participate, and observers may see the entire process of making a shawl, from shearing the sheep and spinning the wool to weaving the shawl.

For the camaraderie of spinners and to keep up with what is going on in spinning, the novice may wish to join a spinners' guild. Spinners' guilds are informal groups, the modern counterpart of the old-time spinning bees, which combined the "sociable" with the feminine (then) chore of making yarn. Today's spinners—men, women, and children, too—get together to spin, talk shop, work on group projects, share information, and to help each other develop spinning skills. Sometimes the spinners' guild is combined with a weavers' guild, but guilds devoted only to spinning are steadily increasing in number throughout the country. If you cannot locate the spinners' guild nearest you, check the registry of spinning guilds, which is published regularly in *Spin-Off, The Magazine for Handspinners* (see below). You will find guilds registered from every state, as well as some in Australia, New Zealand, Canada, England, Ireland, Saudi Arabia, and elsewhere.

Short-term spinning workshops are held from time to time under sponsorship of various spinners' guilds, colleges, craft schools, fairs, restorations, and museums. Sometimes a workshop in another craft, such as dyeing or weaving, is offered at the same time and place. Spinners who attend such workshops make reservations in advance. Membership is sometimes limited and there may be a registration or tuition fee. Workshops usually present general programs, including demonstrations, lectures, contests, and exhibits, as well as sociality. The workshop members often bring their spinning wheels and spin during the proceedings. Spinning workshops are extremely stimulating and worthwhile for both novice and expert spinner. The spinning periodicals are, again, a rich source of information as to places and dates for these workshops.

The beginning spinner who wants individual instruction in spinning can usually find a teacher through one of these groups. Professional spinning teachers sometimes advertise in the valuable spinning periodicals:

Spin-Off, The Magazine for
 Handspinners
310 East Fourth Street
Loveland, Colorado 80537
303-669-7672

Shuttle, Spindle & Dyepot
The Handweavers Guild of America
120 Mountain Avenue, Suite B101
Bloomfield, Connecticut 06002
203-242-3577

WHERE TO BUY HANDSPINNING SUPPLIES

During the last twenty years, spinning has enjoyed a renaissance, and it is no longer in danger of becoming a "lost art." Consequently, there are now plenty of new spinning wheels, spinning accessories, wool and other fibers available on the market, both in the United States and abroad. Many firms carry a complete line of supplies for the handspinner, while others specialize.

Still, there isn't a spinning-supply store on every corner. Most spinners will find themselves at a distance from suppliers and must order many items by mail or telephone.

Remember to send proper postage and a self-addressed stamped envelope when you write to any supplier for prices and information. (Consult your post office about return postage for foreign countries.) I have listed several firms below, as starters. Consult the aforementioned periodicals for additional sources. You can look forward to receiving interesting mail after sending out your inquiries!

FIBERS FOR SPINNING:

FLEECES, COMBED TOP, FLAX,

AND NOVELTY FIBERS

R. H. Lindsay Company
16 Mather Street
P. O. Box 218
Boston, Massachusetts 02124
617-228-1155
$3.00 for sample cards

The Mannings
P. O. Box 687
East Berlin, Pennsylvania 17316
Orders: 1-800-233-7166; catalog $1.00
General supplier

Frederick J. Fawcett, Inc.
1304 Scott Street
Petaluma, California 94952
1-800-289-9276
Specialty: flax and linen

Euroflax, Inc.
P. O. Box 241
Rye, New York 10580

Woodsedge Wools
P. O. Box 275
Stockton, New Jersey 08559
609-397-2212

The Woolery
R. D. #1
Genoa, New York 13071
1-800-441-WOOL
Catalog $1.00

Woolston's Wool Shed
651 Great Road
Bolton, Massachusetts 01740
508-779-5081
Catalog, $2.00 plus SASE
    with $.45 postage

Cotton Clouds
Rt. 2
Safford, Arizona 85546

Creek Water Wool Works
P. O. Box 454
Salem, Oregon 97308
503-585-3302
$3.00 for catalog of
    fibers and equipment

The River Farm
Rt. 1, Box 401
Timberville, Virginia 22853
1-800-872-9665

Fallbrook House
R. D. #2, Box 17
Troy, Pennsylvania 16947
717-297-2498
Silk supplier

Friesel Farm
11510 227th Avenue S.E.
Monroe, Washington 98272
Angora rabbit fiber for spinning

The Silk Tree
Dept. O, Box 78
Whonnock, B. C.
Canada VOM 1So
Samples $4.00

Tarndwarncoort
Warncoort, Victoria 3243
Australia
Phone ISD 001-61-52-336241
Sample cards $2.50 air mail

Carol and Malcolm Dewe
P. O. Box 93
Feilding 5600, New Zealand

Down North
21 Boxwood Crescent
Whitehorse
Yukon, Canada Y1A 4X8
Qiviut

Louise Heite, Importer
P. O. Box 53
Camden, Delaware 19934
1-800-777-9665
Icelandic wools

CUSTOM CARDING

Black Ram Ltd.
5100 Eldora Road
Waterloo, Iowa 50701

Frankenmuth Woolen Mill
507 S. Main Street
Frankenmuth, Michigan 48734

Liberty Ridge
Sunny Bixby
R. D. #1
Verona, New York 13478
315-337-7217
Romney fleeces and angora;
    samples $2.50

SPINNING WHEELS AND ACCESSORIES

Schacht Spindle Co., Inc.
6101 Ben Place
Boulder, Colorado 80301
303-442-3212
List of dealers and catalog, $2.00

Country Craftsman
P. O. Box 412
Littleton, Massachusetts 01460
508-486-4053
Free brochure and list of dealers

Clemes & Clemes, Inc.
650 San Pablo Avenue
Pinole, California 94564
415-724-2036

Crystal Palace Yarns
3006 San Pablo Avenue
Berkeley, CA 94702
Ashford spinning wheel supplier

Louet Sales
Box 70
Carleton Place, Ontario, Canada
613-257-5793
List of dealers and catalog, $1.00

Robin & Russ Handweavers
533 North Adams Street
McMinnville, Oregon 97128
503-472-5760

Newburgh Country Store
Yarn Spinner's Studio
P. O. Box 176
Newburgh, Indiana 47630
812-853-3071

Ertoel Wheels
67 Lusher Road, Croydon
Victoria 3136, Australia

Postscript

Dear reader,

Soon after *The Joy of Spinning* was published in 1971, I learned that there remained still another joy of spinning to be discovered—that of hearing from my readers by letter or telephone. There are so many interesting spinners' stories! Each one is original and yet all have much in common with the experiences I have recounted in my personal spinning story in this book.

Now I look forward to a new generation of spinners who will read *The Joy of Spinning* and have their own adventures. It will be my pleasure if you should share your joy with me in your letters, as I have shared mine with you within these pages.

Sincerely,

Marilyn Kluger
Yarn Spinner's Studio
P.O. Box 176
Newburgh, Indiana 47630

Spinner's Glossary

ACETIC ACID   The acid found in vinegar; used to soften water and to aid in dyeing as a mordanting agent.

ADJECTIVE DYE   A dye that requires a mordant.

ALPACA   The silky wool of the South American llama.

ALUM   Potassium aluminum sulfate, or potash alum; a chemical commonly used as a mordant in dyeing.

ARGOL   Crude potassium bitartrate, or cream of tartar, which is found in wine kegs and can be used for a dyeing mordant.

ATTENUATE   To draw out fibers during spinning.

AXLE   The supporting shaft upon which the spinning wheel revolves.

BAT HEAD   The name designating the wooden, paddle-shaped spindle support on one type of wool wheel.

BATT   The flat layer of combed wool or cotton fibers prepared by hand cards or a carding machine.

BEEDIZI (bā-ē'-dĭz-ē)   The long Navajo spindle, or spinning stick, which is rotated by hand against the leg to spin wool yarn.

BENCH   The table of the spinning wheel on which the large wheel and spinning mechanism are mounted.

BICHROMATE OF POTASH *See* chrome.

BLUE VITRIOL Copper sulfate.

BOBBIN The spool on the spindle shaft of the treadle wheel onto which spun yarn is wound.

BOBBIN PULLEY The small grooved whorl on the spindle shaft of a treadle wheel that connects the bobbin to the driving wheel by the driving band and causes the bobbin to revolve.

BRAKE A device that separates flax fibers from their woody covering by crushing and beating.

BROACH The cone of wool spun on a wool wheel spindle formed on a cornshuck center.

BRUNSWICK WHEEL *See* Saxony wheel.

CARD A wire-toothed brush used in pairs to straighten fibers, as wool, before spinning; to comb out or brush with a card. Also called carder, wool comb, or hand card.

CARDING The process of straightening the fibers and cleaning the trash from wool or cotton fibers before spinning with a machine or hand cards.

CASTLE WHEEL A type of treadle spinning wheel with a flyer and bobbin mounted on a tripod of tall legs, with the spinning mechanism located below the level of the wheel. Known as the Irish castle wheel.

CAUSTIC SODA Sodium hydroxide or "lye"; used as a mordanting agent in dyeing.

CHAIR WHEEL A type of treadle spinning wheel with bobbin and flyer mounted within four chair-type legs.

CHROME Potassium (or sodium) dichromate. An orange crystalline, light-sensitive substance used as a mordant in dyeing. Also called bichromate of potash or bichromate of soda.

CLOCK REEL A reel for winding and measuring yarn into knots of 40 strands after spinning. Also called click reel or wrap reel.

COCHINEAL A brilliant red dye made with the dried bodies of the female of a tropical American insect.

COMB To arrange long wool or flax fibers in a parallel manner by combing in preparation for spinning. Sometimes used interchangeably with the verb "card" in wool handspinning, but refers specifically to straightening long wool fibers for worsted spinning, a process that also removes the noils.

COP The cone of wool formed on a wool wheel or hand spindle during spinning. *Also see* broach.

COPPERAS Ferrous sulfate. A greenish crystalline iron compound used as a mordant in dyeing. Tends to darken colors. Also called green vitriol.

COTTAGE WHEEL Another name for the parlor, or German-type, treadle wheel with bobbin and flyer.

CREAM OF TARTAR An acid, potassium bitartrate, used in white powder form as a mordant in dyeing.

CRIMP The natural curl in the wool fiber.

CROSSBREED The sheep or the wool from a sheep resulting from the cross of two different breeds.

CUT FLAX The length of flax cut from a strip of flax top, prepared for spinning from the hand instead of from a distaff.

DISTAFF A staff that holds the flax or wool fibers, which are drawn from it as needed for spinning. It is secured under the left arm or in the clothing for hand spinning, attached to the spinning wheel for spinning flax, or mounted on its own bench.

DISTAFF SIDE The female line, or maternal branch, of a family. Also, the left side.

DOLLY *See* wheel finger.

DRAFT To draw out or attenuate the fibers for spinning; the length drawn out.

DRIVING BAND The cord carrying the power from the large wheel to the spindle pulley (and bobbin pulley).

DRIVING WHEEL The large wheel that turns the spindle; the "spinning" wheel.

DROP SPINDLE The hand spindle or free spindle that is dropped in front of the spinner while the fibers twist.

DYE OOZE The concentrated dye solution extracted from the dyestuff by boiling it in water.

DYESTUFF Any substance from which dye is made.

EWE A full-grown female sheep.

FAST Refers to a dye color that resists fading.

FELTING The undesirable matting together of wool fibers caused either by high temperature of water used to wash wool or a sudden change in the temperature of the water.

FERROUS SULFATE *See* copperas.

FLAX The textile fiber obtained from the stems of the plants of the genus *Linum*, from which linen is made.

FLAX TOP Flax prepared for spinning in the form of a long, ribbonlike strip.

FLAX WHEEL A low spinning wheel with treadle, flyer, and bobbin, which spins flax and other fibers.

FLEECE The wool shorn from a single sheep; the wool fibers from a sheep's fleece.

FLYER The U-shaped device on the treadle spinning wheel spindle which twists the yarn, once for each revolution, before winding it onto the bobbin.

FOOTMAN   A straight piece of wood or wire that connects the treadle to the axle crank of the spinning wheel.

FOOTWHEEL   Any spinning wheel powered by a foot treadle.

FREE SPINDLE   *See* drop spindle.

FRIENDSHIP WHEEL   A treadle spinning wheel with two flyers upon which two persons can spin at the same time. Also called gossip wheel.

FUGITIVE   Refers to a dye color that fades.

GALL NUTS   *See* plant galls.

GERMAN WHEEL   A common type of upright treadle spinning wheel with flyer and bobbin. Also called parlor, cottage, or visiting wheel.

GOSSIP WHEEL   *See* friendship wheel.

GREAT WHEEL   *See* wool wheel.

GREEN VITRIOL   *See* copperas.

GUIDE HOOKS   The metal hooks arranged on both wings of the spinning wheel flyer which guide the spun yarn as it winds onto the bobbin. Also called hecks or hetches.

HACKLE   To comb flax fibers through a series of hackling combs, or hackles, each with finer teeth, to straighten, clean, and separate the short fibers (tow) from the long fibers (line). Also called heckle, hatchel, hetchel.

HAND SPINDLE   *See* spindle.

HANDSPUN   Yarn spun by hand on a spinning wheel.

HANK   A 560-yard unit of wool yarn wound on a reel. Also referred to as a skein.

HIGH WHEEL   *See* wool wheel.

HOMESPUN   Spun or woven in the home. Also a plain, coarse fabric, formerly made of rough wool or tow and wool.

INDIGO   Any plant of the genus *Indigofera* that yields a blue dyestuff; the dark-blue to grayish-purplish-blue color produced by the dye.

IN THE GREASE   Wool fleece containing its natural grease; also refers to the way fleece still containing the natural grease is spun.

IRON   *See* copperas.

JERSEY WHEEL   *See* wool wheel.

KNOT   Forty strands of yarn wound on a reel measuring two yards around, or 80 yards.

LANOLIN   The natural lubricant in wool; also wool fat, yolk, or wool grease.

LAZY KATE   A bobbin holder used in plying yarns.

LEADER   The length of spun yarn left on an empty bobbin or spindle to facilitate beginning.

LINEN   Thread or fabric made of flax.

LINSEY   Shortened term for linsey-woolsey.

LINSEY-WOOLSEY   A coarse fabric woven of linen warp threads and wool weft threads.

LOGWOOD   An American tropical dyewood used to dye shades of gray, gray-blue, purple, and black.

LONG WHEEL   *See* wool wheel.

LOVER'S WHEEL   *See* friendship wheel.

LOW WHEEL   *See* treadle wheel.

LUKEWARM   Mildly warm or tepid; slightly warmer than the body's temperature of 98.6° F.

MACRAMÉ   A lacework of yarns and threads made by weaving and knotting by hand.

MADDER   An ancient dyestuff from the dried roots of the plant *Rubia tinctorum,* which gives an enduring red color.

MAIDENS   Two upright pieces of wood that hold the spindle of the spinning wheel in a horizontal position. Also called "sisters."

MATTING   *See* felting.

MINER'S WHEEL   A small wheel added to the wool wheel by Amos Miner in 1802 to accelerate the spindle.

MOHAIR   Hair of the Angora goat or the fabric made from this hair.

MORDANT   Any substance used to fix the dye in fibers being dyed or the process of doing this.

MOTHER-OF-ALL   The crossbar that supports the spinning mechanism of the spinning wheel, i.e. the maidens, flyer, spindle, bobbin.

MUCKLE WHEEL   The name by which a wool wheel was known in Scotland. *See* wool wheel.

NIDDY NODDY   Folk name for a simple hand reel used to wind and measure new spun yarn, usually one knot of 40 turns at a time.

NOILS   The short fibers that remain in the comb when combing long wool fibers for worsted spinning.

OAK GALLS   *See* plant galls.

OOZE   *See* dye ooze.

ORIFICE   The opening, or eye, of the spindle on a treadle spinning wheel.

OVERTWIST   Refers to excess twist in spun yarn.

PARLOR WHEEL *See* German wheel.

PLANT GALLS Abnormal growths on leaves and branches of trees, especially oaks, caused by insects, which contain tannin and are used as a mordant or dye.

PLY To twist two or more yarns together.

POTASSIUM BITARTRATE *See* cream of tartar.

PULLEY A small grooved whorl carrying the driving band from the large driving wheel to the spindle of the spinning wheel.

QIVIUT (kiv'-ē-ĕt') The fine, soft, silky, long-fibered wool underfleece of the musk ox.

RAMIE A woody Asian plant producing a flaxlike fiber in the stem.

RETTING The process of rotting the flax plant in water, as in a flax pond, or by dew retting.

RIPPLING The process of removing the seeds from the flax plant by pulling it through a ripple.

ROCK An old term meaning the distaff, from the German *Rocken*.

ROCK DAY An ancient English holiday observed on January 7, when the Christmas respite from the task of spinning ended. Also St. Distaff's Day.

ROLAG A narrow roll of combed wool prepared for spinning; also called sliver.

ROVING A long, continuous rope of combed fleece prepared for spinning. Also rove.

SADDEN A dyeing term meaning to darken the color, as iron does.

SAXONY WHEEL A treadle spinning wheel using Johann Jurgen's flyer and bobbin, originating in Saxony (northwestern Germany) in the 16th century, which changed spinning from an intermittent to a continuous process. Also called Brunswick wheel, after the German city where Jurgen lived.

SCOUR To wash wool free of grease and dirt.

SCUTCHING Process of beating or breaking flax with a scutching knife and flax brake (or break) to separate the outer woody fibers from the inner textile fibers. Also called swingling and braking.

SIMMERING POINT A temperature just below the boiling point of 212° F.

SISTERS *See* maidens.

SKEIN A unit of spun wool wound into a loose, elongated coil, usually consisting of 7 knots, or 560 yards. Also called a hank.

SKIRT To remove dirty and defective wool from the outer edges of the shorn fleece.

SLIVER   A continuous strand or rope of carded wool, or the product of the card.

SLUBS   Irregularities or lumps in spun yarn.

SPEED WHEEL   *See* Miner's wheel.

SPINDLE   (1.) A spinning stick weighted with a whorl, or disc, that is used to spin fibers by hand. Also called hand spindle, free spindle, drop spindle. (2.) The part of a wool wheel upon which yarn is spun and wound. (3.) The part of a treadle wheel bearing the bobbin and flyer upon which yarn is spun and wound.

SPINDLE PULLEY   The small grooved whorl that carries the driving band connecting the spindle to the driving wheel.

SPIN   To draw out and twist two or more fibers together to form a continuous yarn.

SPINNER   Anyone who spins, male or female.

SPINSTER   A woman who spins thread; also a woman who does not marry, an "old maid."

STANNOUS CHLORIDE   *See* tin.

STAPLE   Refers to the length of a lock of shorn wool.

STRICK   A bundle of flax prepared for spinning.

STITCHERY   Contemporary needlework using yarn and large embroidery stitches to make designs on cloth.

S-TWIST   The twist in yarn spun when the wheel turns counterclockwise, or a right-twisted yarn.

SWIFT   A reel used to hold yarn as it is wound off.

TANNIN   Tannic acid used as a mordant in dyeing.

TABLE   The bench of the spinning wheel, which supports the wheel and spinning mechanism.

TEASEL   A plant of the genus *Dipsacus* from which the bristly flower head was obtained to disentangle, or "tease," wool fibers. Used also in fulling cloth and called fuller's teasel.

TEASING   The precarding process of loosening the fibers in a lock of fleece by passing it from one hand to the other, a bit at a time, without pulling the fibers apart completely.

TENSION   The tautness of the driving band on the spinning wheel.

TENSION SCREW   The device for controlling the tautness of the driving band of the spinning wheel.

TIN   Stannous chloride; a mordant used with other substances in dyeing. When used with alum to make color brilliant, the process is called "blooming."

TOPS   Long-staple wool fibers for worsted spinning, which are prepared by combing out shorter fibers. Also a commercially prepared wheel of wool roving, ready for spinning.

TOW The short fibers left after flax is combed.

TOW FORK A distaff with forked prongs set around the top of the staff for holding tow roving for spinning.

TREADLE The foot pedal of a spinning wheel that turns the main wheel; the process of working the treadle.

TREADLE WHEEL A spinning wheel powered by a foot treadle; a footwheel.

TWIST The entwining of two or more fibers to make a single strand; the spinning motion and its effect.

WALKING WHEEL Common name for the wool wheel, given it because the spinner walks back and forth while spinning.

WARP The lengthwise threads in woven fabric.

WEFT The filling, or crosswise, threads interlaced through the warp in woven fabric. Also woof.

WETTED WOOL Wool that has been presoaked in water.

WHEEL FINGER A wooden stick about 9 inches long used to turn the spokes of the wool wheel; also called a wheel dolly or dolly.

WHORL At first this applied to the weight put on the end of a spinning stick to help it spin; later it came to mean the small fly wheel that regulates the speed of the spinning wheel spindle.

WOAD Ancient dye plant that produces a blue dye.

WOOF *See* weft.

WOOL The thick, soft, often curly hair of sheep and other mammals.

WOOLEN Made of wool. The method of spinning short-staple wool fibers.

WOOL WHEEL Common name for the large, hand-turned, wheel-driven spinning wheel with a simple spindle that spins wool yarn; also walking wheel, long wheel, great wheel, high wheel, Jersey wheel, muckle wheel, etc.

WOOL POOL A depository for wool fleece produced under a government-subsidy program.

WORSTED Woolen fabric made from long-staple fibers; first made in Worstead, England. The method of spinning yarn from long-staple fibers.

YARN The product of spinning short fibers together to make a long, continuous strand.

YEARLING A young sheep, aged one year, that is ready for the first shearing.

YOLK *See* lanolin.

Z-TWIST The twist made in yarn when the spinning wheel is turned in the clockwise direction; a left-twisted yarn.

Index

ABOUT THE AUTHOR

Marilyn Kluger is a native of Evansville, Indiana, and a graduate of Indiana University. Her interest in needlework sparked *The Joy of Spinning*. The native dyes she uses for her handspuns—and discusses in her book—reflect her fascination with natural things and particularly with useful wild plants. She collects them—for food, for dyestuffs, for her wildflower garden—in the woodlands and meadows of Indiana and on family vacations in Vermont. The many uses of wild plants in cooking are the subject of *The Wild Flavor*, also from Henry Holt.